WITHDRAWN
UTSA Libraries

WITHDRAWN
UTSA Libraries

ROTHSCHILD RELISH

ROTHSCHILD RELISH

by
RONALD PALIN

CASSELL · LONDON

CASSELL & COMPANY LTD
35 RED LION SQUARE, LONDON, WC1
Melbourne, Sydney, Toronto
Johannesburg, Auckland

© Ronald Palin 1970
All rights reserved. No part of this publication
may be reproduced, stored in a retrieval system,
or transmitted, in any form or by any means,
electronic, mechanical, photocopying, recording
or otherwise, without the prior permission of
Cassell and Company Ltd.

S.B.N. 304 93515 8

First published 1970

Printed in Great Britain by
Ebenezer Baylis and Son, Ltd.
The Trinity Press, Worcester, and London
F.1069

Contents

Acknowledgements

Several former colleagues have helped me by refreshing or supplementing my own memories of the old New Court. I am most grateful to them all and to Jack Bennett, Herbert Elton, Peter Hobbs and Leo Kelly in particular.

For much of the information in Chapter 2 about the early history of the site I am indebted to Philip E. Jones, Deputy Keeper of Records of the Corporation of London.

The lines from the Halton song 'Beech Leaves' are quoted by kind permission of the Commandant, Royal Air Force, Halton, and with acknowledgements to Lieutenant-Colonel R. Kingsley-Pillars, O.B.E., and R. H. Cort.

Chapter 1   **Many of the Accidents**

The words 'New Court' were nowhere visible and there was no name-plate or other indication that this was the office of N. M. Rothschild & Sons. It was evidently something that everybody knew; everybody, that is, except the schoolboy of seventeen who in the summer of 1925 was applying for a job. There was just a high archway opening off St Swithin's Lane through which a cobbled courtyard could be seen. I might have noticed the red shield projecting over the lane but the five arrows and the motto *Concordia Industria Integritas* which appeared on it conveyed nothing to me nor were the entwined gilt letters NMR easily decipherable from below.

Under the archway stood a large man wearing a bowler hat, blue serge suit and highly polished black boots, who looked like a retired policeman. He confirmed that this was the place I was looking for, courteously but with an undertone of sternness from which it was clear that I should not be admitted without a good reason. I had an appointment with Mr Archer, I told him. He raised his hand to his hat and directed me to a door on the far side of the courtyard.

Inside the door two or three smaller and less formidable men also in blue suits were sitting on a bench. One of them took me up a narrow flight of uncarpeted wooden stairs to the first floor and into the presence of Archer, the Staff Manager.

He was a middle-aged Irishman with a face as white as his collar and he sat at a massive old-fashioned desk with his back to the fire-place in a room overlooking the courtyard. The distempered walls were covered with photographs and Spy cartoons. After being reminded of the circumstances in which I had been introduced to the firm by Sir Gordon Nairne, a director of the Bank of England and a friend of a friend of my father, he examined the School and Higher Certificates which I had received from the Oxford and Cambridge Schools Examination Board. He then asked me if I could spell correctly the words 'parallel' and 'acknowledgement', which I could and did. That matter having been satisfactorily cleared up he took me downstairs to see Mr Lionel de Rothschild.

Since I was not applying for a post of major responsibility it struck me as slightly peculiar that I should be interviewed at the top level. I did not realize in what a very personal way this very personal family business was run. The whole staff numbered well under a hundred and no clerk was engaged in even the humblest capacity without first being seen by one of the partners.

At that time the two brothers Lionel and Anthony de Rothschild, great-grandsons of Nathan Mayer Rothschild, the founder of the firm, were the only partners. They remained the only partners for the next fifteen years. The contingency had then to be considered that both of them might be killed in the same instant by the same bomb, with results for the future conduct of the firm too hideous to contemplate. So a corporate partner was formed, with no other function but to take over the control of the business in such a terrible eventuality. But in 1925 it was Lionel and Anthony; the firm was the two of them and they were the firm; in them resided all power and what they said went.

I followed Archer's black-coated back respectfully downstairs, into the buzzing General Office and up to the door of The Room. Some of the rooms at New Court had names which indicated what went on there, such as the Bullion Room or the humbler filing-room or the posting-room (which did not have anything to do with the post); others went by the name of the occupant or the occupant's occupation, like Archer's room or the butler's pantry; yet others were described by reference to their location, like the one which was never called anything but 'the little room at the top of the back stairs'. But the room in which the partners sat was always called simply 'The Room'. The smaller one which they had used until 1860 and which was the only part of the building to survive the major reconstruction which then took place, had become the 'Old Room'.

Archer peered through the glass upper half of the door, received a signal and went in. I followed.

It was a large and lofty chamber, about forty feet long and with a high moulded ceiling. Glossy oak panelling of a rather ugly yellow colour covered the walls to the height of eight feet, above which was white plaster. At each end was a fire-place and a black marble chimney-piece. It was a room which was to play a large part in my life until it, too, was demolished with the rest of the building in 1962. It was many years before I felt wholly at ease in it.

The principal articles of furniture that I took in on that first entrance were two huge mahogany writing-tables with brass edges and leather tops into which were let panels of bell-pushes. The nearer one was untenanted, for Anthony was absent that day from the office. Behind the other, at the far end of The Room, sat Lionel, in an armchair with a cane seat.

He was smoking a cigar. From that first meeting until the day in 1941 a few months before his death when I said good-bye to him at Tring before leaving for Washington, I never saw him without a cigar in his mouth or between his fingers.

We advanced towards him across the vast expanse of thick Turkey carpet and were invited to sit down in armchairs upholstered in dark reddish-brown leather. He beamed at us, his geniality always to the fore on such occasions, and spoke of Sir Gordon Nairne; he showed no surprise at learning that my introducer did not actually know me although we had friends in common. I intimated that I would certainly like to come to New Court but I added, with a resolution only slightly weakened by the glamour of the surroundings, that I rather wanted to go first to Oxford, to which it was thought that I might get a scholarship.

Lionel said two things which I remember. The second, which seemed reasonable and acceptable, was: 'It'll be ten years before we know whether you are going to be any use to us or not.' This remark was never alluded to subsequently. But before that he said: 'If you want to come, you'd better come now.'

It had always been taken for granted, when the subject of careers came up during my childhood, that I would try to get into the Royal Navy by way of Osborne or Dartmouth. Ships and the sea were my first love; my second, fostered by the masters who taught English at Rossall, was literature. Even as a schoolboy I was enough of a realist to regard the latter as a spare-time pursuit from which I could hope to derive lasting pleasure, mental satisfaction and spiritual refreshment, but hardly a regular income. The idea of a naval career, on the other hand, was only abandoned when it was discovered, rather belatedly, that I was barred from it by the irremediable barrier of short sight.

When this condition had been recognized and corrected by spectacles the wonder and delight with which I looked at a world never seen clearly before dimmed my disappointment. Figures on the stage or the blackboard stood out for the first time in sharp focus. All things became bright and beautiful as the misty obscurity of a Turner sea-scape crystallized into the clarity of Canaletto. But the question inevitably arose: what was I going to do? I had no idea. Certainly the thought of merchant banking, or even of ordinary banking, never occurred to me.

My father was Canon Residentiary and Precentor of a small cathedral. Or rather, that is what he ought to have been; what he was in fact was an official of the Bank of England. He was intended by nature to be a parson but life made a *manqué* of him. I have a picture, not the less convincing for being completely imaginary, of him living quietly and happily in the close with his garden and his piano, his pipe and his books, officiating every afternoon at evensong and endearing himself to all the old ladies by his clear tenor voice and ascetic appearance. He was tall, lean and clean-shaven and was careful to keep his bald pate always decently sunburnt.

But he obtained, by what was considered great good fortune, first a nomination to a post in the National Provincial Bank and shortly afterwards a transfer to the Bank of England, which he served faithfully for forty years. Most of that time was spent in the old Western Branch of the Bank in Burlington Gardens, in the office which later became the Royal Bank of Scotland. Three years before his retirement in 1934 he was moved to the head office in Threadneedle Street, but I think he always felt that if banking were your lot it was better to practise it in the West End, a quarter of London which he felt to be rather more gentlemanly than the City and one in which you met a better class of customer.

As a member of one of the best amateur operatic societies in the south of England he was familiar with the works of Gilbert and Sullivan and in particular with the lines:

> The shares were a penny
> And ever so many
> Were taken by Rothschild and Baring. . . .

Apart from that it is doubtful whether in 1925 the name of Rothschild meant very much to him. But when in the course of discussions about my future the possibility of an introduction to N. M. Rothschild & Sons was mentioned he soon realized that this might be a 24-carat opportunity. Every knowledgeable person to whom he spoke said that, with the possible exception of the Bank of England itself, Rothschilds were regarded as the best employers in the City.

He could no doubt have arranged for the doors of the Bank to be opened to me. That he did not do so was due, I always supposed, to the fact that his own career, one for which he was not temperamentally suited, had been undistinguished and to a consequent belief that his young hopeful might do better elsewhere.

5

Lionel's invitation to 'come now' was exciting and alarming at the same time: exciting because my first sight of New Court had already filled me with a desire to work there; alarming because I was not ready for it. I did not want to forgo a last year at Rossall, when I should have been fagged for as I had once fagged; I did not want to forgo the prospect of becoming a school monitor and of winning the annual prize for reading the lessons in chapel, if no other. More importantly, I did not want to sacrifice three years at the university. I wanted to rub ideas with superior intellects and discuss Brancusi and Pareto, knowledge of whom was then the mark of the highbrow, or at least Aldous Huxley and D. H. Lawrence; I wanted the two letters after my name which friends whom I did not consider much cleverer than myself had managed to achieve.

Why then did I say 'yes' to Lionel? It is hardly enough to point out that he was a difficult man for a coeval to argue with, let alone a boy of seventeen. In any case he did not say positively that it would be no good my coming back after four years; only that there was a job for me now, while nobody could tell what the situation would be then. It is hardly enough to say that my father was under some financial strain and would be glad to be relieved of some of it; or that against the prospective joys and intellectual rewards of a university I set the vision of a salary and a freer life; or that I was dazzled by a name and a building and an atmosphere. Anyway, after reflection, I did say 'yes'; and then the row started.

In my first year at Rossall the school had gained a record number of open scholarships to Oxford and Cambridge. To mark the occasion we were all given a whole holiday, an event which sticks in my memory not only because it occurred very rarely but even more because on that day, in the back seat of a 'sharabang' in which I was returning from Lake Windermere with other members of my house, I had my first sexual experience, at the hand of an older boy. It was something which happens sooner or later to many, perhaps most, boys at public schools and although memorable was quite harmless and unimportant.

After that outstanding year constant efforts were made to equal or break the record and boys who had come to Rossall with a scholarship, as I had, were relied upon in particular to get, or at least to sit for, scholarships to one or other university. When it was announced that I was going to leave it was felt that I was letting down the side as well as wastefully failing to complete an education which was considered to show promise. My friends pleaded with me and my masters shook their heads sadly; the headmaster, finding persuasion useless, became so angry that he threatened my father with legal proceedings for the recovery of my scholarship moneys. My father had signed a paper in which he noted that I should be 'expected' in due course to sit for a university scholarship; his solicitors argued that this language did not constitute a binding obligation and the headmaster was compelled reluctantly to agree. In sorrow and anger he let me go.

All this argle-bargle had the effect of reinforcing my conviction that I was right. During the holiday weeks of waiting I felt more and more elated at the prospect of getting down to a job after nine years of boarding-school; not, moreover, any old job but one with a firm of whose prestige and renown I was daily becoming more aware. It was not until much later that I began to realize what I had missed and to feel the ache which has been alternately assuaged and sharpened by the *splendeurs et misères* of life at New Court but has never completely left me.

On 29 September 1925 I entered the service of N. M. Rothschild & Sons at a salary of £100 a year. I would have to wait a month, of course, for my first salary cheque but on 30 September I was presented with an envelope containing four one-pound notes as one month's 'lunch money'. £48 a year represented such a high proportion of my total emoluments that to spend it all on lunches seemed recklessly extravagant. It was only very rarely during those early years that I expended as much as three and sixpence at the White Hart in Cannon Street on a meal which comprised a fillet steak grilled before my eyes by a man in white called Henry, two vegetables, half a pint of beer, cheese and biscuits and coffee.

7

After I had been at New Court a few months I received another envelope containing a cheque for about £4 which I was told was my share of something called 'poundage', a mystery not solved until I went to the Dividend Office. At the end of the year the day came when Archer put a hand on my shoulder, leaned over me and wrote '£20' on my blotter. It was his customary way of imparting the news that one had been given a rise.

I have attempted to convey in a light-hearted manner something of the unique flavour of life at New Court in those days and something of the nature and atmosphere of that awkward, inconvenient but strangely lovable building. I have drawn on memories; mine and those of friends who can look back even farther than I can. The book is about myself without being an autobiography; about N. M. Rothschild & Sons without being a history of the firm; and about some members of the Rothschild family without being another book about 'the Rothschilds'.

Not only is it not a history of the firm; it is not even a history of it during the past forty years. No secret details of financial operations will be revealed, no account attempted of the inner workings of a famous merchant bank and its place in the economic life of the nation, no assessment offered of the power and influence of the firm in *weltpolitik*. So much must be said at the beginning, both to avoid disappointing those who still eagerly await such a serious history and to re-assure the greater number whom it would fail to amuse.

For an autobiography, of course, it would be as difficult to find an excuse as for another volume on the exhausted subject of the Rothschilds, their wealth and how they spent it, the figures they cut in society, their houses and estates. If I had been tempted to engage in such an exercise I should have been effectively warned off by certain reviewers whose remarks might have been aimed deliberately in my direction. 'Autobiography,' said one, 'is the most difficult of prose forms, especially when the author has no achievement to record much more than growing up.' Another found it hard to understand why anyone, except for vanity or spite, should want to write an autobiography, a form which a third considered was only for the self-important, the sour and the disgruntled, not the contented.

So I have tried to write of my own doings only in so far as they took place within New Court, and if I have strayed sometimes beyond its walls it is to tell of events outside which arose directly or indirectly from preceding events within and so may illumine a small corner of the picture.

For it is really of the old New Court that I wish to write; of the old New Court and of some of the characters for whom it was not just an office but a club and a second home. And I want to do so not just because to me they were fascinating but because the old building and the spacious life that was lived there, both of which might have been specially designed to encourage the cultivation of eccentricities, have gone for ever.

This was the old New Court which had scarcely changed for sixty years; this the way of life which had probably remained the same for even longer. This was the New Court where I worked and played and composed topical doggerel for the notice board; where I ate and drank and occasionally slept; where I was by turns happy and miserable, exhilarated and frightened; where I met good men and bad, charming nonentities and dull celebrities, beggars and multi-millionaires, statesmen and tycoons and the boys with brains who laboured obscurely but indispensably in the back rooms of the world. But it was the gaiety and excitement which I remember.

Among the bibelots in The Room which I barely glanced at during my first audience was one that I often studied with delight on subsequent occasions. Framed and glazed and mounted on a small brass stand it occupied a place of honour on a side-table. It was a letter to the father of Lionel and Anthony from Disraeli.

My dear Leopold, [he wrote from Hughenden Manor on 11 December 1880] I found your telegram on my return from Windsor yesterday. It gave me the greatest pleasure.

There is nothing so happy as a happy marriage, and I

9

feel, that yours will be such, for, while you command many of the accidents which contribute to the felicity of life, you possess those personal qualities, which are the indispensable elements of domestic happiness: good sense, good temper, and that intelligent and adequate experience, which make companionship delightful.

I have not yet the pleasure of knowing the lady, yet I will presume to offer to her my kind wishes.

Besides, my dear Leo, I have always been of opinion, that there cannot be too many Rothschilds.

Yours sincerely,
Beaconsfield.

Chapter 2 Don't You Wait

I began, as our founder did, with bills of exchange.

Nathan Mayer Rothschild (who will be referred to here as NM, as he always is at New Court, the initials NMR standing for the firm) was only twenty-one when he arrived in Manchester in 1798, the third of the five sons of Mayer Amschel von Rothschild of Frankfurt. Although he was very far from being penniless or friendless it would be difficult even for one who does not regard skill in handling money as the highest expression of human genius to deny, in the light of his achievements during the next few years, that he must have possessed outstanding abilities.

William IX, the Elector of Hesse Cassel, had given NM full power to deal with that portion of his fortune which was invested in British Government securities and later on further very substantial sums belonging to the Elector and other German princes were placed at his disposal through his father Mayer Amschel. After ten years he had built up such a reputation that he was entrusted by the government of George III with the transmission of remittances for Wellington's army in the Spanish peninsula and the payment of subsidies to various allied continental rulers.

Nevertheless it was as a dealer in cotton and cotton goods that the young man started in business in Manchester. His book of samples, containing snippets of cloth in a variety of colours and designs, is preserved at New Court as one of the firm's most treasured relics of its historical beginnings. In common with the founders of the other great merchant banking houses NM was a merchant first and a banker afterwards. With the transition to banking we come back to bills of exchange.

These are the pieces of paper, founded on credit, by means of which the movement of goods all over the world was and still is financed. When NM bought raw cotton from abroad he did not pay for it by taking gold pieces out of his pocket. He paid for it by accepting, that is to say guaranteeing the payment at maturity of, a bill of exchange drawn on himself by his supplier. In a surprisingly short time he had acquired such a reputation for integrity that his name on a bill made that bill as good as cash; everybody recognized it and nobody refused it.

But other merchants, who knew and were known by NM, had not the same reputation and the same facility. They came to NM and said: 'NM, do me a favour. You know me. If I say I'll pay I'll pay. But I'm not well enough known generally. Put *your* name on my bill and then everyone will know that it'll be paid at maturity.' 'Certainly,' said NM, 'but who's talking about favours? I shall have to charge you a commission.'

They agreed on terms and the deal was done. That was the point at which NM changed from a merchant to a banker. In 1804, the year of the firm's foundation, he moved to London and established himself in Great St Helen's. In 1809 he moved finally to New Court, St Swithin's Lane, which became both his residence and his office and has been the address of NMR ever since.

It is an address as familiar in the circles in which I have spent my life as Buckingham Palace or No. 10 Downing Street; so familiar that one easily forgets that in much wider circles it means nothing at all. What actually was New Court and why was it so named?

St Swithin's Lane is a short, narrow thoroughfare, permitting only a single line of traffic, which runs north from Cannon Street to a point close to the Mansion House, the Royal Exchange and the Bank of England. New Court was originally a small square on the west side of the lane with a large house on its north side, smaller houses on the other sides and two or three shops on the street adjacent to the great gate of the mansion.

In the fourteenth century the big house was owned by the eminent legal family of le Scrope. It passed to one Roger de Depham, Alderman of Candlewick and Recorder of the City. He lived there until his death in 1359 and bequeathed it to the Mayors, Aldermen and Commonalty of the City. The site has remained continuously in the possession of the City Corporation ever since.

The medieval mansion was occupied by a succession of mayors, aldermen and other City dignitaries until it was destroyed in the Great Fire of 1666. It was rebuilt and shortly afterwards the name New Court came into use, although even then the courtyard was certainly very old. In 1720 it was rather repetitiously described as a 'very handsome large place with an open passage into it for coach or cart. Here are very good buildings and at the upper end is a very good large house enclosed from the rest by a handsome pale.'

Some repairs were necessary in 1793 when the lease previous to NM's was granted and these give some idea of the character of the place when he entered into occupation. It had 'a cantilever cornice, a covered colonnade on the south side with steps up to the front door, a brick parapet, cock-loft, garrets and flats; within there were marble chimneypieces, kitchen, scullery, warehouse and counting-houses'.

Such was the property of which the lease was assigned to NM in March 1809. Later he took a new lease from the City for twenty-one years from Christmas Day 1815 at a rent of £175 per annum, which was double that paid by his predecessor. During the years that followed the firm gradually acquired other properties both within New Court and on St Swithin's Lane. When the office was rebuilt in 1860 the frontage had increased to one hundred feet and the rent to £1,000 per annum. The process of expansion continued; in 1899 the firm acquired No. 7 St Swithin's Lane for £8,000 and some years later conveyed it to the Corporation. In this way the freehold of the whole site was consolidated in the Corporation and it is now held by NMR on a single lease—at a rent, it is hardly necessary to add, considerably greater than that which was considered appropriate a hundred years ago.

While he was still in Great St Helen's NM had not been too busy founding a great bank to found also a dynasty. In 1806 he had married Hannah Barent Cohen; in 1807 the first of his seven children, Charlotte, had been born and in 1809 his eldest son, Lionel, who was to become known as Baron Lionel and to succeed his father as head of the firm. In 1809 the growing family was not too large to be installed in the house which was also thenceforward the banking house and one can well imagine the energy with which NM, still only thirty-one, set about adapting New Court for both purposes.

At the same time he was busy expanding the business and making himself well known not only in the City but in the financial world. New fields were rapidly being conquered and new activities developed in addition to the financing of imports and exports and the movement of goods with which the story began. But to this day the financing of trade by means of acceptance credits remains one of the two principal functions of the merchant banks. The description is applied loosely to a number of institutions, but it ought properly to be confined to the sixteen or so who are members of that exclusive body known as the Accepting Houses Committee.

One day at lunch when we were discussing the movement of goods about the world a client who was present told us about a certain much-travelled consignment of sardines. 'It was bought in Portugal,' he said, 'and shipped to London. There it lay in a warehouse for a while before it was sold to a chap in Hamburg and shipped there. The German sold it to a firm in Italy and he exported it to somewhere in South America. After that it was consigned, I think, to Scandinavia and then, if my memory is correct, to Germany again.' At that point one of us felt bound to interrupt. 'I wonder,' he said innocently, 'that after all that the sardines were still fit for human consumption.' 'Consumption?' said our client; 'my dear sir, those sardines weren't for eating, they were for buying and selling.'

At New Court, as in most organizations which deal with them, bills of exchange were handled by two separate departments, one for Bills Receivable and one for Bills Payable. The bill payable was drawn on us and presented to us for acceptance; the bill receivable was drawn on somebody else, sent to us by our client and presented by us for acceptance. Movement of goods was always involved. The job of the presenter was to satisfy the acceptor, by documentary evidence, that all the conditions had been complied with, that the goods were the right goods and had been shipped in the right ship, at the right time and to the right consignee and destination; the job of the acceptor was to accept the bill and so in effect make it almost as good as cash.

The great expert on acceptance credits in my young days was Philip Hoyland, an amiable man and a most faithful and loyal servant of the firm. I never ceased to be amazed by the extent of his expertise and the amount of work he got through personally. But he was no classical scholar. The occasion is often recalled when he was discussing a certain shipment on the telephone with another bank. 'The ship,' he said, 'is the S.S. Mean Louse. . . . What? Mean Louse, man, Mean Louse!' His voice became louder and angrier. 'Damn it, it's written here on the bill of lading in black and white: m, e, n, e, l, a, u, s.'

But I myself was placed in the Bills Receivable department. Prior to my arrival it had consisted of only two men, Theo Rhys-Jones and Hugh Miller. Theo, the head, must have been about sixty and he retired shortly afterwards. Hugh, though he also seemed an old man to me, was very much younger. He was engaged on a book, *The London Foreign Exchange Market*, which was published the following year and he also enjoyed some fame in the horticultural world, in particular as an expert on irises.

The kindness and patience which those two displayed towards the new recruit was traditional and normal at New Court, but it was nevertheless impressive and memorable. They were very busy; the quantity of bills coming in was considerable, and they needed help. What they got was a youth who thought himself well-educated but whose ignorance even of the most elementary commercial matters was total.

They started me off numbering and entering bills in a book called the 'S' book. First I had to number the bill with a heavy brass numbering machine.

Like my father before me I have never been completely at ease with anything mechanical and I had trouble with these machines from the first day. There was a whole battery of them on the shelf for bills of various series. In the hands of a skilled operator, or even an operator who was not afraid of them, they worked perfectly well; but even when I understood them they still made me nervous.

The drill was that you took the bill to be numbered and selected a clear space on it where the number would not obscure some piece of essential information. You then, in order to deaden the noise, interposed a thick rubber mat between the bill and the desk-top, which was sloping. The machine, which was about seven inches high and covered an area of about two square inches, was then placed over the chosen site and held firmly in position with the left hand; with the right hand you grasped the ebony handle at the top and depressed it rapidly and firmly—down and up again, quick and easy. The inking pad in contact with the numbering barrel moved aside; the barrel came down, left its mark on the bill and returned, encountering on the way back a tooth which turned it to the next number. You replaced the apparatus on the shelf, ready for the next time, and there on your bill was the number neatly printed: S4097. If all had gone according to plan you would then find that S4097 was the next open number in the S book, in which the numbers had been pre-printed.

People who go downstairs again after they have got into bed to make sure that a hot-plate has not been left on in the kitchen, or who when half-way to the station return to the house in case the front door was not properly shut, will at once comprehend the unsatisfactory nature of this simple process, which had the terrifying irrevocability of a posted letter. The trouble was that you could not tell, by inspection of the state of the machine, what number it would print next, and so satisfy yourself that that number was indeed the next open number in the book. You could, of course, number a piece of blotting paper first but in doing so you automatically clicked up the next number. You could also move a little lever which had the effect of making the machine print each number twice before clicking up the next, and that was often useful when you had to number firsts and seconds of exchange together, that is to say your original bill and its duplicate which sometimes came into your hands together. But that involved remembering to move the little lever before your trial run and to move it back afterwards. It was a long time before I could simulate the manner in which after long practice Theo Jones and Hugh Miller would bang numbers on bills without, it seemed, ever doubting for an instant that they would be the right ones and appear clearly in the right places.

Extremely expensive adhesive bill-stamps had next to be affixed to the bill and cancelled. Unless there was any other process I have forgotten they were then ready to be presented to the drawees for acceptance by the 'walks' man. At that time he was old Ridgway—called old simply to distinguish him from his son, young Ridgway, who later became the head of the Records Department. Old Ridgway looked so much as though he ought to have been exercising horses on Newmarket Heath rather than walking the streets of the City that I was not at all surprised to hear that he had been coachman to Mrs Leopold. He had once allowed the horses to run away and although it was only a minor accident in which nobody had been hurt it was thought safer to transfer him to New Court. He was always neatly and soberly attired, as were all the porters and messengers, in a blue serge suit and a bowler hat; not for NMR the brass buttons of some bank messengers, still less the pink coats, red waistcoats and silk hats sported by those of the Bank of England. Later in the day the bills would be brought back and Theo Jones or Hugh Miller, having examined them to see that they had been duly accepted, would put them away in the

Strong Room where they would lie until maturity, when they were brought out and presented for payment.

The bills had also to be entered by me in a diary under their due dates. Unfamiliar with the vertical ruling of cash-books, I entered my first batch with the thousands figure squeezed into the same column with the next three instead of being put out to the left. Cecil Lovering of the Control Department came in due course to check the book and tick my figures in the green ink reserved exclusively for his department. He was a member of one of the many New Court families of those days, both his brother and later his nephew being also on the staff. I shall never forget the gentle courtesy with which he pointed out the error of my way. 'It does make it rather difficult for the chap who has to make the cast, and if you wouldn't mind . . .'

We became friends and the following year, during the General Strike, he gave me lifts to the office in his car.

Another of my jobs was to enter in a large book all the esoteric details of the weekly return of the Bank of England, from which old Ridgway used to collect a copy every Thursday. I was also made responsible, naturally under close supervision, for making and receiving the sterling payments due as a result of the transactions of the Foreign Exchange Department. This task was carried out by Bills Receivable owing, presumably, to their convenient proximity to the cashiers and the counter.

These were all simple and comprehensible chores, but not so simple that I made no mistakes. Theo Jones, among his many lovable and admirable qualities, was an artist with the scratcher. This was a special kind of knife about six inches long supplied by William Neely & Co., our stationers. It had a wooden handle with a two-edged blade which on one side was straight and could be used for sharpening pencils or peeling apples and on the other had a semicircular bulge like a dorsal fin. This was, for me, by far the most useful tool in the office. Its use was demonstrated by Theo as soon as the need arose, which naturally it did before I had been at New Court more than a few hours, for a figure incorrectly entered by me in ink had to be erased. You grasped the semicircular blade of the scratcher firmly with two fingers on one side and the thumb on the other, holding it low down for maximum control. Then, with the lightest possible touch you scratched back and forth rapidly but gently across the offending figure. If you pressed too hard you went through the paper but if you were careful you would find after a few minutes' patient scratching that you had just removed a tiny area of surface. When all trace of ink had disappeared you had to restore the gloss to the area before inserting the new figure, otherwise the ink would run. This you could do by rubbing the spot with the middle finger-nail pressed on to it by the thumb. Such was the quality of the hand-made paper of which our ledgers were expensively composed that a skilled operator like Theo could alter a figure in this way quite undetectably.

Banging, stamping and scratching I passed the first day. Towards six o'clock Theo Jones said: 'Don't you wait.' It was his invariable formula. 'Don't you wait, Palin.' I didn't, then. That came later.

Chapter 3   **The Best Club in London**

'This, my boy,' said George Tite, warming the seat of his elegant Edwardian trousers at the coal fire in the General Office, 'is the best club in London. We really ought to be paying a subscription instead of receiving a salary.'

It was two o'clock in the afternoon. George, art-critic, connoisseur and collector, a dandy, a clerk in the Correspondence Department of NMR and a rich man who had made a great deal of money by 'stagging' the firm's Russian loans which always opened at a premium—George was holding forth to a small group which was not excessively keen to get back to work. With his high collar and stock, his black jacket and narrow striped trousers, his thin cynical smile and his mordant wit, he typified the now vanished New Court dilettante.

At his back the fire blazed brightly; between him and it a screen of wire mesh was interposed for the safety not so much of members' trousers as of valuable papers. Above, on the brown marble mantelpiece at the level of his head, the directories of Kelly and Didot-Bottin were placed for ready reference. Higher still was the great clock which could be seen, or for that matter watched, from every part of the General Office; actuated, I always supposed, directly from Greenwich Observatory, a pair of regulating pincers would emerge from its face precisely at noon and squeeze the hands together at top dead centre.

Along the wall to George's left were two chests, one containing drawers full of stationery, the other the brass-mouthed letter-box. Members of the staff at that time enjoyed the privilege not only of using the firm's writing-paper, die-stamped with the New Court address but without the firm's name, for such private letters as they found time to write in the office, but also of dropping them into the firm's box and having them stamped with the firm's stamps.

Directly opposite where George was standing, on the other side of the big office, was the door into The Room. The upper half of it was glazed so that every time you passed you could look in and see one or other partner at work at his desk—and nearly always both of them. At this moment the green blind had been drawn down behind the glass indicating that the partners were at luncheon and that it was the Children's Hour.

On his way to New Court that morning George had dropped in at Christie's, where by chance he had met Anthony de Rothschild. They had a look round together and at about a quarter to eleven Anthony looked at his watch. 'Well, I must be getting along to the office.'

'Ah,' said George. 'Well, good-bye then, Mr Anthony, I'll see you later.'

George's grandfather had been harbour-master at Dover at the time of the Battle of Waterloo. In that capacity he may well have been of some assistance to NM's courier who reached New Court with news of the victory twenty-four hours before Wellington's own emissary arrived at Downing Street. Possibly this service was in Anthony's mind when he refrained from drawing George's attention to the propriety of keeping regular office hours.

In the fullness of time George had arrived, looked at his mail and started to compose his letter to the Brazilian Government, his own pet client, whose financial agents the firm had been for a hundred years. Now he was digesting an excellent lunch preparatory to completing the letter, which he wrote in copying ink in his own spidery but clear and legible handwriting. It reported every transaction, every debit and credit, in that important client's very active accounts: *nulla dies sine linea*. By about four o'clock it would usually be finished. 'We have the

honour to remain Your Excellency's most obedient servants . . .'
To others fell the chores of checking, initialling, signing, copy-
ing, enveloping, stamping and posting this daily missive:
George Tite went off to his other club.

'You boys may chide me for arriving so late,' he said, although
of course we should not have dreamed of doing so, 'but allow
me to point out that by the time I get here I have bathed,
shaved, breakfasted and crapped. Other people may get here at
ten, but if ever I am here early I notice that they then immediately disappear for about an hour, presumably for just those
purposes.'

'Mr Tite,' one of us asked, 'what did you think of the cigars
which the Rue Laffitte sent us?' The French house, de Rothschild Frères, was often referred to metonymically by the street
in Paris in which the office was situated. A special job had
recently been completed for them and some cigars had been
sent over for distribution among the clerks at New Court who
had had to work late on it.

'Well, I'll tell you,' said George, delighted at the opportunity. 'I thought they were exactly right.'

'Exactly right? Do you mean—?'

'I mean they were exactly right,' George repeated. 'If they
had been any better the Rue Laffitte wouldn't have given them
to us and if they had been any worse we couldn't have smoked
them.'

Monsieur Magneval—the Marquis de Magneval, some said,
though whether this was a real or just a courtesy title I never
knew—came into the General Office. This cadaverous-looking,
kindly Frenchman had arrived at New Court in 1911 shortly
after the Sidney Street battle and was christened Peter the
Painter because of his supposed resemblance to one of the protagonists. He became the firm's principal French correspondent,
but even after living in England for many years and marrying
an English wife he never succeeded in mastering the pronunciation of our language.

Now he approached the group and George Tite pretended
not to see him. 'As I was saying, I personally would never

travel by sea except on a French ship. A French ship for me always.'

Monsieur Magneval came up. 'That's very nice, George. I am delighted. Do you mind telling us why?'

'Not at all, my dear fellow. The reason is that in the event of disaster there's never any of that damn nonsense about women and children first.'

One of our number knew the next move, which was calculated both to change the subject and to display the Marquis's idiosyncratic pronunciation for our enjoyment. 'How are your birds, Monsieur Magneval?' he asked. 'What have you got in your aviary at present?'

In his abundant spare time the Marquis was a clever designer of book-plates and monograms, but it was well known that his main interest outside the office was caged birds and that he could always be drawn on this topic.

'My birds, yes. I have—let me see—a cannaree, a leenay and a boulle-fansh. So beautiful!' He pronounced all three words as though they were French.

'Tell Palin about the two luminous points, Monsieur Magneval.'

He obliged without hesitation. 'Two small lumineuse pwants. There they were on the road in front of me as I was driving home late one night. And what do you think they were?'

'Another car?'

'No!'

'Two motor-bikes?'

'No, no!'

'What, then, Monsieur?'

'I will tell you. It was a howl eating a mice.'

At this point a torrent of tinkles was heard from every part of the General Office as all the green glass lamp shades—there was one above every desk—were tapped repeatedly with rulers or pen-holders. Callon, the Chief Cashier, had returned after a lunch lasting two hours to a demonstration organized by Theo Jones, who for some occult reason disliked him. This was quite a common method by which the inhabitants of the General Office would mark their approval or disapproval of a colleague's behaviour and it appeared sometimes to break out quite spontaneously. Nor was it always restricted to the Children's Hour; on one occasion the noise drew Anthony hastily out of The Room in the belief that the office was on fire. History does not record what explanation was offered to him, which is a pity, for I am sure it was highly ingenious.

In the present instance Theo had not only warned me that the demonstration was coming but had delighted me by the gentle and diffident manner in which he pointed out the impropriety of my taking any part in it.

But now the Children's Hour was over; we returned to our desks; the partners came back from lunch; the green blind was raised. Most of us, who had work to do, got on with it. Some calculated that they could not go downstairs for a cup of tea for at least an hour and a half; others considered gloomily that it was a long time to six o'clock; others, whose early night it was, reminded their neighbours gleefully of the fact. And Mr Ziffer began to check letters.

This was a spectacle which I watched fascinated. It was, of course, an important process which he was carrying out; every letter which went out was subjected to it. Although the bottle-neck was narrow the flow of letters was small enough for passage through a central checkpoint to be still feasible.

Ziffer was an Austrian by birth and was reputed to be a Count. Like Tite he was a member of the Correspondence Department but unlike Tite he was always busy and always in a hurry. He did his job very thoroughly, holding up each letter as he checked it three inches from the thick lenses of his spectacles; so thoroughly, indeed, that he always began with the die-stamped address. 'New Court, St Swithin's Lane,' one could hear him reading to himself in a soft whisper if one were near enough. 'Yes, that's right. London, E.C.4. Right.' Then he passed on to the date and from that to the body of the letter, which he also read under his breath but quite audibly. If the letter were ready for posting he would put it into its envelope, hesitate for a moment and then suddenly withdraw it in order to check the contents all over again.

He was usually among the last to leave. Anyone else still about could hear him clatter down the stone steps to the washroom with a noise like an early machine-gun and a few minutes later observe him rush off to the station, generally wearing a long ulster which flapped about his ankles. In winter he carried a very large lever-operated torch to light his way across the fields to his house. I was told that he invariably put on a dinner jacket before dining with his wife, after which he sat reading the *Financial Times* until it was time for bed. 'They tell me I have a very pretty wife,' he said once. 'I really don't know—I never see her by daylight.'

Ziffer was one of several linguists whom the firm then employed. Many letters from the firm were written in French in those days; many were received in German, Spanish and Portuguese also. There was thus always a demand for and nearly always a supply of men competent in foreign languages. Sometimes the supply was more than adequate: one man who had been engaged because of his knowledge of Italian complained that in all his years of service he used it only once, and that was when he was sent to Victoria Station to meet a new Italian maid for Mrs Lionel de Rothschild.

What I had expected to find when I went to New Court straight from school, I don't know. I had no standards of comparison and no knowledge whatever of banking or commerce. Most probably my mind contained no clear picture at all of what went on in this or any other merchant bank; certainly none which bore the remotest resemblance to the actuality which revealed itself during those early years. I could not have anticipated that I would find an organization which on the one hand was obviously efficient, successful and profitable yet which on the other appeared to be managed largely by amiable eccentrics who did very little work and that without much seriousness and by antiquated methods. There was an explanation, of course, but I discovered it only gradually and not until later.

But even then the winds of change had begun to stir the air, winds which were to increase steadily in strength until by the nineteen-sixties, blowing at gale force, they had demolished the very building itself and left untouched by their violence nothing save the memories and emotions and skills of a handful of survivors.

In 1915, ten years before my arrival, when Leo Kelly, who was to be my predecessor as Secretary of the firm, joined the staff at an even more immature age, a mild and almost imperceptible zephyr had not gathered strength enough to do more than put one typewriter and four or five telephones into the office. Like mine, his entry was the result of a personal introduction, in his case to that same Leopold de Rothschild whose marriage inspired Disraeli to such flights of hyperbolical fancy. The fact that they were both called Leo formed a bond upon which that most genial of bosses did not fail to remark. Like mine, Leo Kelly's father had made inquiries and been told by a bank manager that NMR were 'the envy of the City'. This young innocent, too, upon whom it had been impressed that he was entering the greatest financial house in the world, found that the organization and methods were very different from his expectations.

What was it like, that New Court, that stone fortress into which those two wide-eyed boys were admitted?

The building was the second that the firm had occupied on the same site. Passing under the great red shield with the five gilt arrows and the Latin motto, you entered the cobbled courtyard through the high archway which was closed at night and at week-ends by heavy mahogany doors; entered it, that is to say, if you were not stopped by the so-called policeman at the gate. He had been a real policeman and on retirement from the force had been employed by NMR to direct persons on their lawful occasions and exclude undesirables. The new clerk, if he was well advised, would introduce himself to the big bowler-hatted man and try to become his friend.

Set in the south wall of the archway itself was a door leading on the left to a small office called the French room because it had been used to accommodate visitors from the Rue Laffitte, and on the right to the porters' 'lodge' where the nightwatch-men kept their unceasing vigil.

New Court was built round the west, north and east sides of the courtyard. Facing you, on the west side, was the only major part of the original building which remained after the recon-struction of 1860. This was the Old Room, one storey high with three windows separated by Corinthian columns. Above its roof you could see the upper windows of the Dividend Office, of which it was part; to the left of it was the door to the Bullion Room, entirely separate from the rest of the office and entered only that way, and to the right, at the top of a short flight of steps, the clerks' entrance. On the north side were the windows of The Room and in the north-west corner the partners' entrance, naturally larger and more imposing than the other, approached up shallow curving steps and with the glass-panelled doors of mahogany instead of oak. To the right of the archway, facing west across the courtyard, was the single large window of the partners' dining-room. Against the high south wall which separated New Court from Salters' Hall stood the couriers' box, a sort of wooden shed like a cabman's shelter in which the 'outside' men sat.

The New Court couriers were a remarkable body of men. They were recruited for the most part in the Folkestone area; many of them were descendants of the mariners who manned the cutters used by the firm in its early days to convey agents and despatches across the Channel. They stood ready to carry messages anywhere at any time; one day a man might have only to walk round to Bishopsgate, the next to leave at five minutes' notice for Budapest. Once in every eight days each man did a spell of forty-eight hours' consecutive duty, for twenty-four of which he went without sleep. Every night two men remained on the premises: one, called the watchman, stayed on the alert and received any incoming cables or tele-phone calls; the other went to bed but was aroused if a message had to be delivered, for example, to a partner's town house.

Also on duty at night was a fireman—not actually a professional fireman, as he had once been, but the man who patrolled the whole building in case of an outbreak of fire.

The couriers were all men of infinite resource, considerable sagacity and commanding presence but none possessed these qualities in such high degree as one called Paul, who was said to hold a master's ticket. He always carried a loaded revolver when he was on duty at night or at the week-end but relied on his fine voice, his height and his air of authority to get him in anywhere the partners sent him, no matter what sort of barrier was put in his way. He had such a strong sense of security that he would conceal from strangers who had no business there the very nature of the building, and when rubbernecks wandered in asking 'What's this place?' he would always tell them that it was the stables of the Mansion House.

Paul also possessed a strong sense of the hierarchical grades of New Court and became very angry if any of his juniors appeared to ignore them. One day when a courier nodded and smiled in friendly response to a greeting from a young clerk who had only been on the staff a few days Paul marched over and issued a stern reprimand. 'I saw you just now treat that young gentleman in an offhand manner. Just you remember, my lad, that he is a clerk and you are a porter. As long as he and you are both at New Court, whenever he deigns to speak to you you will address him as "sir". Get it? Sir always.'

The partners' entrance was used by the partners and those having business with them; the clerks' entrance was used by everybody else. This, at any rate, was the theory; in practice the rule was not applied with great rigidity. It was not true, so far as I know, that any clerk caught sneaking in by the wrong door was flogged in a sound-proof basement room, although it may well have been that a warning of that kind was given to new entrants. For that matter they were also told that a rather rusty sword, a relic of the Peninsular War, which used to hang in a glass case in the front hall, was kept for the purpose of operating upon such of them as were found not to have been circumcised.

Let us now, however, without prejudice, continue our tour of the old building by going in at the *entrée des patrons*. Passing through two pairs of heavy swing doors, partly glazed, we find ourselves in the square, panelled and thickly carpeted front hall, where, if we are visitors, we shall be received by one of the front-hall men. These were a race of men entirely different both from the outside men and from the back-hall men whom we shall meet later: without exception family retainers of many years' standing, some translated from one or other of the private houses, they were older, more dignified and more intimidating than their counterparts at the other door, and by comparison with the rugged and breezy couriers they were pale and delicate. Their suits were the same dark blue and made by the same tailor in St Swithin's Lane, but their coats were of the morning or cutaway type. They were devoted single-mindedly to the interests of the partners, whom they protected from undesirable intrusion with suave inflexibility. No gentleman's gentleman in fact or fiction, it seemed to me, could surpass the dignity and polished manners with which they carried out their duty of receiving the caller, relieving him of his hat, coat and umbrella, seating him with *The Times* in the waiting-room, announcing him and conducting him into The Room; and at the end of the interview, of helping him into his coat, brushing it, restoring the gloss of his top-hat, opening the door for him and seeing him safely down the steps.

One major-domo whom I remember with particular affection was a short, round-faced and completely bald man called Ruddle. The respect with which I treated him from the first bore fruit later when, on occasions when I changed into evening dress in the office, he would undertake to polish my own silk hat for me, a task to which he brought unrivalled expertise. Some of the senior porters used to be given allotments of stock when the firm issued loans; unlike most of the others, who immediately sold theirs, Ruddle held on to his and when he died, unmarried, he left his niece a fortune of several thousand pounds.

To your left as you entered the front hall was the door of

The Room; before you was the door into the General Office, over which in winter hung a heavy curtain of some dark red material with a unique capacity for attracting the ubiquitous dust; and to the right was the open way through to the partners' waiting-room.

The gloom of this windowless chamber was compensated for by its atmosphere of Victorian solidity and respectability. It contained a large writing-table with a silver ink-stand from which projected two little-used but decorative quill pens, mahogany chairs upholstered in dark red leather and also, by the time I got there, the lift and the tape-machines. The latter were three in number: one ticked out general news, one Stock Exchange prices and the third racing results and other items of a sporting nature. There was a rack for hats and coats and umbrellas on one wall and against another stood a high desk for those who preferred to make notes standing up. Inside it, under the sloping lid, reposed a large handsomely bound book containing the name, private address and telephone number of every member of the staff.

If we cross this waiting-room, turn right outside it, ignore the wide uncarpeted stone stairs on our left leading up to the first and second floors and down to the basement, and advance a few paces to another tall oaken door, we are following the route of the partners and their guests to luncheon. Into this lofty oak-panelled room, with its huge single window looking out on to the courtyard, and its long table which when fully extended would seat twenty people, have come the kings, princes and governors to whom, however exalted their station, lunch at New Court, as much for its ritual and ceremony and social significance as for the excellence of its food and drink, was a memorable occasion. At the time we are describing no clerk was ever invited to lunch with the partners; the category included the entire staff from the general manager, who in fact used to be called the chief clerk, downwards. It was not until much later that the freshening wind blew a whiff of democracy into the office and from time to time a senior employee was invited into luncheon with the partners.

As an instance of the rigidity of the class division at the old New Court the story is told of a day when Lionel de Rothschild was conferring with Philip Hoyland and a solicitor, Hugh Quennell, a partner of the firm of Slaughter and May. At one-thirty Lionel rose from his desk. 'Come and have some lunch, Quennell,' he said. 'Hoyland, you'd better go and get your dinner.'

Hoyland was sufficiently amused by this language to recount it, but it didn't surprise him or us. To anyone today who finds it distasteful rather than funny I would point out that it merely reflected with complete accuracy the attitude to his own world which had been bred into Lionel from his birth. Later in his life he gave his friendship warmly and unreservedly to Henry Bevington, who succeeded Archer as Staff Manager and Chief Accountant but was, of course, still a clerk—an employee. It was a totally different Lionel who invited Bev to play golf with him and admitted while they were walking round the course that he had always had too much money for his own good and that everything had come to him too easily. He had no experience and very little knowledge of life as it was lived by the great majority of people in England but he was well aware of his ignorance and so far from attemping to hide it he appeared to me sometimes to delight in exaggerating and exhibiting it. Many of his remarks which I heard or heard of and shall recount here seemed to me to be simply instances of Lionel de Rothschild playing the part of Lionel de Rothschild and consciously portraying him larger than life.

It is true of course that he was temperamentally disinclined to mix with the common people and it was convenient for him that the life to which he had been born made it unnecessary for him to do so. I doubt whether he ever in his life travelled by bus or underground. In this respect he differed from his brother Anthony, who, when he was going to his country house near Leighton Buzzard, would insist upon taking the tube from the Bank station to Euston. Sometimes this insistence bordered on the morbid. When he was carrying home a suitcase or some large parcels his secretary, Eve Icely, would tell him firmly that he was no longer a young man and should really take a taxi. 'All right,' said Anthony, 'send a porter in a taxi with the luggage. I'll go by tube and meet him at the other end.'

Chapter 4 **Ah, the Darling!**

If you went in by the clerks' entrance and proceeded straight ahead, passing the door of the Old Room on your left, you found yourself in the Dividend Office. In terms both of space occupied and bodies employed the group of departments which went by this traditional but rather inexact description comprised almost half of the entire office. Here it was that in 1915 Leo Kelly was first put to work counting and cancelling coupons. Here Peter Hobbs and Michael Bucks, arriving on the same day in 1924, began in equally humble jobs the long climb which was to bring the former to the position of Investment Manager and the latter via the General Manager's seat to the historic achievement of one in The Room, when he became the first member of the staff to be taken into partnership. I myself was not put into the D.O., as it will be convenient to call it, until after I had spent five years in other departments, but when I was it was at a higher level and without having enjoyed direct experience of the lowly chores which my illustrious precursors had learned. Since I remained a member of the D.O. for the next thirty years (I regarded myself as still a member even while on secondment elsewhere during World War II) and was head of it for the last thirteen of them, this was perhaps a pity. However, if I made any mark at all upon New Court it was in the D.O. There will therefore be more to be said later about this side of the office. For the moment we shall ignore it and turn right into the back hall.

This was really little more than a passage from the clerks' entrance to the General Office. Here you would find, seated on a bench on the left, a squad of blue-suited back-hall porters or messengers. In the years between the wars New Court was among other things peculiar in its enjoyment of a higher proportion of non-clerical to clerical staff than existed in any other institution in the City. In front of the porters' bench, high on the right-hand wall, was a large indicator showing where any of the forty or so bells was pushed anywhere in the building.

These men, if you arrived early enough in the morning, could be seen in aprons and shirt-sleeves polishing the brasswork and bringing up ledgers from the book-room where they reposed for safety over night. For the rest of the day they were engaged in fetching and carrying. They also filled ink-wells from a gallon bottle.

From the back hall, in an aperture in the wall opposite the men's bench, a narrow enclosed flight of wooden stairs led up to the first floor. At the end of the corridor a right turn past the head of the stone stairway leading down to the basement brought one to the waiting-room, the General Office counter and beyond that the General Office itself. This was a long, lofty, windowless room into which daylight penetrated only through the skylights high above. The Room, which adjoined it, and the General Office were the heart or focal point of the organization: for all the years when the partners and the general manager thought it essential to be, and be seen to be, always in the midst of things.

Banks in the City of London today, even merchant banks, whose clientele is different, receive their public in surroundings of great magnificence. The idea of a City bank conjures up in the mind's eye a vista of lofty elegance and restrained splendour, of wide polished floors and soaring marble columns, and one can sympathize with the woman who on the opening day of a new head office building was found kneeling at prayer beside one of the pillars in the belief that she was in a cathedral. In particular, of course, one pictures a long counter with a bronze grille of handsome design and the finest workmanship behind which suave experts stand ready to pilot customers through the fearsome financial jungle in which they unconcernedly dwell.

A young City man of today, if one could re-create the past for him and lead him up to the public counter in the General Office of the old New Court, might well say, as strangers sometimes did, 'Is this a bank?' He would find it odd, in the first place, to have to pass through the back hall, which was not calculated to impress him or even make him feel welcome. The little waiting-room adjacent to the counter was comfortless and even somewhat alarming, since there was a cut-out section in the middle of the wooden floor. It is related, indeed, that one evening about closing time an impatient client who felt that he was being neglected and happened to be standing incautiously on this section of the floor thumped it with his stick and was promptly lowered into the basement as he stood, the man below believing that he had been given the signal that the account books which were usually piled there at that hour were ready to be put to bed.

Although there was indeed a counter, surmounted by a grille, it was unexpectedly short and narrow, with little about it to impress the caller with the fact that he was in a banking house of historic fame and standing at the point of contact between its officials and the public. The office beyond the counter, on the other hand, with its great height and glossy oak panelling, did have a sort of elegance and the visitor's eye would certainly be caught by the handsome carved pediments over the doors symmetrically placed in the corners at the far end.

It has to be realized that merchant banks did not and do not have large numbers of private customers with current accounts and cheque-books as the joint-stock or clearing banks do. NMR had a few such accounts and they issued cheque-books, but for the most part their account-holders were members of the family, who did not transact their business across the counter, or commercial firms who for various reasons might find it convenient to have a current account and a cheque-book in connection with other facilities, like acceptance credits, which the firm was extending to them. Many people have thought from time to time, and still do, that it would be pleasant to have an account with NMR and to pay their regular tradesmen's bills with cheques drawn upon such a distinguished banking house, but unless they were rich enough to maintain a very large balance on current account or were personal friends or connections of the partners they were not accepted. It was pointed out to them with perfect politeness and truth that this policy was dictated not by snobbish reasons but by the simple fact that the firm was not equipped to handle this type of business and that they would do better to go to one of the clearing banks which were.

Naturally exceptions were sometimes made for certain individuals who were neither related nor very rich, particularly if they appeared in the *Almanac de Gotha*. If the King of Barataria or even the Duke of Plaza-Toro wanted an NMR chequebook he generally got one and our books certainly contained the names of a number of majesties, highnesses and dukes both arch and grand. The correspondents told me that in their youth they remembered one eminent client called the Duc or the Marquis d'O—his full title—and that the staff were always fascinated to see letters or cheques signed by him with that single letter.

Although some of the firm's *hochwohlgeboren* clients occasionally came in personally to draw money—one who always appeared for this purpose on his visits to London was the Prince of Monaco, father of the present Prince Rainier—the rather poky General Office counter was used in the main by bank and other messengers. On the left of it was the Stock Department's guichet. Behind it sat the cashiers and the men who dealt with bills payable and bills discounted; adjoining them in the same block was the section devoted to bills receivable. This section consisted of four high sloping desks at right angles to the counter, all joined together like a terrace of houses. Beyond these departments a lateral passage-way divided them from the rest of the General Office; from that a carpeted corridor led down on the right past the door of The Room and the door into the front hall to the managers' corner at the far end, while on the left another ran past the fire-place and the mail box to the Cable Department in the corner, the filing-room and the room of the Foreign Exchange Department.

Blocks of desks likewise joined together in 'terrace' formation filled the space between the corridors, from which each department was entered by a door five feet high of which the upper half was glass. On each side was a row at which the clerks sat on high chairs, their feet under the sloping desk tops on foot-rests, those on one side having their backs to those on the other, leaving a passage between. Above each man's head was the green-shaded lamp, horizontal rails on which he kept his books and a narrow brass plate screwed to the partition bearing the important but not always heeded legend 'please make as little noise as possible'. The whole central part of the General Office formed an enclave surrounded by mahogany partitions.

When Leo Kelly arrived in 1915, having been engaged by Leopold through his secretary, Carl Nauheim, there was only one typewriter in the whole office and that was very little used. Nearly all letters were written by hand in the Correspondence Department, which was situated in the central part of the General Office. Joseph Nauheim, Carl's brother, who was the manager but was called the chief clerk, was also head of the Correspondence Department, which he supervised from a dais fifteen inches high.

Set in the panelling on the right-hand wall of the General Office, close to the door of The Room, was a cupboard containing its only telephone. Any clerk having occasion to use this instrument, including the chief clerk himself, had to open the cupboard door and stand with one foot inside on its raised floor and one outside in the passage. The cupboard was still there when I appeared but by that time contained only hooks for the hats and coats of a few senior men who did not wish to use the common racks below stairs.

There was one other telephone in the small room at the end of the office which became the filing-room, but that was not available for the clerks because the room was used by the Hon. Charles Rothschild and known as 'Mr Charles's Room'. All the telephones, including those on the partners' own desks, went straight through to the City exchange as there was no switchboard in the office.

Those were days when the serious business of the office was done by a handful of men who did most of the thinking and felt all the anxieties. The remainder of the staff led lives which were for the most part free from cares and pressures. They usually had plenty of spare time and when they were busy it was with work which they knew so well or was of such a simple and undemanding kind that it occupied only their hands and left their minds and tongues disengaged. It was, at New Court, the heyday of the practical joker, that peculiar animal whose activities, sometimes entertaining but more often tiresome, belong to a more leisurely age.

The practical jokes perpetrated at New Court ranged from the harmless to the nasty and from the simple to the highly elaborate, from those which raised a quick laugh and were soon forgotten to those which must have rankled for months. Most were childish, some ingenious. Nobody minded very much, after carrying home what he thought was an exceptionally heavy Christmas turkey, when he found a large lump of coal at the bottom of the basket. Much more unpleasant was the practice once or twice indulged in of threading a hair through the length of a cigarette with a needle, with the result that the smoker was made violently sick after a few puffs. I find it difficult to imagine who in that friendly office can have been disliked enough to be the victim.

A slightly less malicious affair was organized for a notorious lady-killer, one which required the co-operation of half the staff of the General Office and the expenditure of money as well as time. A small advertisement, purporting to have been inserted by a girl who was intrigued by his reputation but had not met him, appeared in the personal column of his usual newspaper conveying an invitation to him to respond through the same channel if he was interested. He did so, and a series of messages of increasing warmth ensued. Finally it was proposed by the other party that they should meet outside Cannon Street station at lunch-time, when our man was to identify himself by wearing a white flower in his button-hole. When he turned up he found a dozen or so of his colleagues at the trysting-place all with gardenias in their lapels.

An even more elaborate example of misdirected energy and inventiveness occurred when a case purporting to contain twelve bottles of sherry was delivered to a man in the D.O. as an anonymous gift requiring only the handing over of one pound for delivery charges. As anticipated the beneficiary smelt a rat and refused to pay up, whereupon a colleague offered to accept the consignment and the expense himself. The case was then opened and the single genuine bottle of wine in it withdrawn and passed round. When a similar case arrived a few weeks later addressed to the same man he accepted it gladly, carried it home and found twelve carefully prepared bottles full of water.

It is time we had a look at the old partners. The first Lord Rothschild had died a few months before Kelly joined, leaving a legacy of a year's salary to every member of the staff, and the partnership then comprised his two younger brothers, Alfred and Leopold, his younger son Charles, and his nephew Lionel, Leopold's eldest son. Charles's older brother, Lionel Walter, succeeded to the title, but he was a naturalist and not a banker. Charles himself did not play a very active part in the business, although he was keenly interested in the gold-refining side of it, and neither at that time did Lionel, who as Major de Rothschild was working as recruiting officer for the City of London in an office on the other side of St Swithin's Lane.

Alfred never married. The gay bachelor of the family, he had a few years earlier celebrated—in this instance the misused *mot* is, I feel confident, *juste*—his seventieth birthday, and such was the volume of congratulatory letters and telegrams which fluttered in from all parts of the world that the staff of the Correspondence Department had to be kept late one evening to acknowledge them. As the time passed one, whose name has come down to us, Dr Kalisch, began to fidget until finally, at about seven o'clock, he could keep silent no longer and pleading an important dinner engagement begged his colleagues to release him. They agreed to do so but resolved to make him pay for it. Accordingly the next morning they greeted the doctor with cries of simulated sympathy. 'Hope you enjoyed your dinner party,' they said, 'but what rotten luck; you had scarcely gone before Mr Alfred came out of The Room and gave each of us ten pounds.'

Dr Kalisch's agony can well be imagined. He moped and fretted the whole morning. By the time Alfred arrived he had screwed up his courage to the requisite pitch and into The Room he marched.

'Good morning, Mr Alfred.'

'Morning, Kalisch,' said Alfred interrogatively.

'I was one of the men who were working last night on your birthday telegrams.'

'Yes?'

'I thought you would like to know, Sir. Unfortunately, I was obliged to leave a few minutes earlier than the others.'

Alfred waited for the point with raised eyebrows.

'So I wasn't there when you came out, Mr Alfred. I felt in the circumstances you would want me also to have ten pounds like the others.'

Alfred's main desire must obviously have been to terminate this totally incomprehensible conversation as quickly as possible. Looking across The Room he observed that his brother Leopold was watching and listening. He concluded that there was only one thing he could decently do.

'I don't understand what this is all about, Kalisch,' he said, 'but anyway here is ten pounds for you. I hope that is satisfactory.'

The interesting point to note about this incident is that the protagonist believed unhesitatingly that Alfred had indeed handed out a tenner apiece, because that was the kind of thing that did happen. In the prosperous days before 1914, in addition to annual bonuses, called 'touchings', presents were often given at Christmas and for summer holidays, and tips were sometimes handed out on birthdays and other anniversaries. A man would announce to the partners that it was his silver wedding, and be rewarded with twenty-five sovereigns; another would mention with an elaborately casual air that he had just completed thirty years' service with the firm and emerge from The Room richer by that number of good pre-war pounds. Some men would contrive by this sort of means to double their basic salaries, which in any case were by the standards of the period not small; and when it is realized that the relatively negligible income tax then levied on their emoluments was also paid by the firm it will be easily understood that our predecessors of sixty and seventy years ago sometimes seem to us to have been on velvet. But it was not a good system: it was not a system at all, for it was haphazard. The ones who asked were the ones who received. The practice was abused by those with too little pride and scorned by those with too much, and its inevitable demise should not be regretted.

Senior members of the staff certainly lived in a style which their sometimes envious latter-day successors cannot begin to emulate, but it was as nothing compared with the magnificence in those days of the Rothschilds themselves. So much has already been written about vast estates, armies of servants, palatial mansions and lavish entertainments that no description of them need be attempted here; we are, in any case, concerned principally with New Court. But it may be noted that these 'accidents', to use Disraeli's word, did not arouse envy; the staff, to whom the family were a race apart, observed them from a distance with vicarious pride and pleasure.

For Alfred and Leopold indeed, the two partners who in 1915 were most in evidence, all their clerks had great affection. The genial Leopold in particular, who was responsible for staff matters and to a great extent acted as his own staff manager, was much loved. With a kindness and humanity which have descended in a large measure to his grandsons he devoted himself to the welfare of the clerks, not so much as a duty or in a spirit of *noblesse oblige* as because it was in his character to do so.

41

Especially in times of ill-health or other adversity was his generous concern manifested. One man, suffering from a chest complaint, was sent by Leopold to Switzerland to recuperate and later to Australia for six months; another, distraught by the death of his wife, was given a trip by sea round the world. It was the custom of all the clerks who were free to do so to watch the brothers' arrival from a convenient window, since their manner of ascending the steps was regarded as a barometer of their health. After Leopold had been unwell Kelly would hear voices (of other Irishmen, one suspects) saying 'Ah, the darling, I think he is looking a little better today'—or words to that effect.

Paternalism had not then acquired its later pejorative significance and Leopold's staff rewarded him with a loyalty to his family and himself which, with its good name, remains the firm's greatest strength and asset. Whenever I looked at his portrait and discerned so clearly in his painted features the character of the man, I felt that of all the ancestral voices his was the one I would most wish to have heard myself.

It is easy to understand, and even at this distance in time to share, the feeling of horror with which the staff heard that an attempt had been made on Leopold's life. One morning as his car turned in under the archway a crazed Jewish student ran towards it pointing a pistol. The plain-clothes policeman on duty, whose name was Charles Berg, sprang forward and struck the youth's arm just as he fired, with the result that the bullet intended for Leopold penetrated Berg's own neck. He recovered in hospital and although Leopold offered to give him a pension for life he chose to remain with the firm and became a courier.

Alfred was whisked by car from his house in Mayfair to New Court in a manner hardly excelled by any member of the Royal Family. A policeman, seeing him leave, would signal to another at the end of the street and the word was passed along the route. Traffic was held up where necessary so that his progress should not be impeded and if there were an obstruction the driver would not hesitate to avoid it by passing islands on the wrong side. At New Court the man at the gate, warned by telephone, was on the alert to spot either partner's car as soon as it turned into St Swithin's Lane from Cannon Street and at his whistle all the six or seven couriers on duty lined up in the courtyard. At that time a fire-engine manned by two men was stationed permanently in the yard and the firemen would fall in too. When the car drove in under the archway the firemen sprang to attention and saluted, the couriers raised their bowler hats with almost military precision and one of them stepped forward to open the car door.

Leopold arrived first at about eleven o'clock, lunched at half-past one and left at about five. Alfred did not turn up until two o'clock or later, lunched between half-past three and four and after his brother's departure often fell asleep on a leather-covered sofa.

This sometimes created a problem for certain members of the staff who could not leave until all the day's letters had been signed. Every letter had to be signed by a partner, since 'per procuration' signatories did not exist at that time; it was after six o'clock, the letters were ready, the remaining staff wanted to go home and the only partner on the premises was fast asleep. What was to be done? Ingenuity, never lacking, found a way. There on the mantelpiece was Kelly's Directory, a large and heavy volume which, raised to head height and dropped once or twice just outside the door of The Room, could usually be guaranteed to do the trick.

The habit of napping on that sofa, hard and uncomfortable though it was, seems to have persisted and to have continued to cause trouble. Peter Hobbs's father, W. B. Hobbs, who was Secretary of the Union Discount Company and a familiar visitor to New Court, was appealed to one day just before closing time when a seven-figure cheque which was expected from NMR failed to arrive. Knowing the partners well he offered to run round to New Court, where he found that the cheque was un-signed and the only partner on the premises asleep on the couch. The directory technique was varied on this occasion and a nervous and reluctant front-hall man was persuaded to open and slam the door of The Room until the untimely slumber within was dispelled.

It seems to have been unthinkable to walk in and rouse the sleeping partner by the simple and direct method of a hand on his shoulder.

Chapter 5　**Leave Monday till Tuesday**

After a year in Bills Receivable I was transferred to the Cable Department, in which most young New Courtiers did a spell sooner or later. It was situated in a corner of the General Office close to the General Manager's desk and watchful eye and to the door into the Foreign Exchange Department.

It may be noted that the day had not yet come when it was felt appropriate for the General Manager and his assistants to have a room to themselves in which they could enjoy a certain amount of seclusion and interview their frequent visitors in privacy and comfort. Samuel Stephany, the incumbent at the time of my arrival, sat on a high chair and at a high sloping desk no different from those of junior clerks in the General Office. He could, it is true, withdraw with a caller to a small waiting-room a short distance away, but many are the directors and senior executives of major companies who recall with wry amusement having to stand beside Steph's desk to talk to him or perhaps to sit with him on a hard and narrow wooden bench along the wall.

Both sites were, of course, in full view of everyone in the General Office and it was George Tite who, seeing the senior partner of the Swiss banking firm of Paravicini Christ & Co. on the bench with Steph on one side of him and Philip Hoyland on the other, could not forbear to say: 'Look, there is Christ between the two thieves.'

Young clerks would either be posted to the Cable Department

for six months or a year, as I was, as part of their general training or were put on the early morning cable roster. This was an arrangement under which a couple of juniors from other departments came in an hour earlier than the rest of the staff to open and decode the large number of cables which had been delivered out of office hours and prepare them for distribution. The telex system had not been introduced then, nor was the long-distance telephone in such regular and constant use as it is today, so that the volume of cable traffic was considerable in a bank which did a great deal of foreign business. Codes, whether public such as those of Petersen and Bentley or private, were much used for secrecy and economy. Since the airmail was not so rapid and reliable as it has since become, a young man 'doing cables' would soon get a pretty good idea of almost everything that was going on.

One bright spark in Bills Payable on one occasion made excellent use of the knowledge of procedure which he had acquired in this way when he realized with consternation that he had mailed to Cairo a set of shipping documents which should have been sent to Buenos Aires. Without a word to anybody he walked round in his lunch-hour to Cannon Street Post Office and despatched at his own expense a telegram to the firm's correspondents in Egypt, using the correct inter-changeable telegraphic address so that the message appeared to have emanated officially from NMR, expressing regret for the error and requesting that the documents be sent back by airmail without delay. There was also an early morning post roster; our friend made sure not only that he was on it for the next week or two but also that he was the first of the squad to arrive. In this way he was able in due course to intercept the returning packet and re-direct it to the proper quarter without anyone knowing anything about it.

It remains to be added that he did in fact tell the whole story to his chief—but not until several years later, when the only possible reaction was one of admiration for his resourcefulness.

Frank Roberts was the head of the Cables Department, John

Cockshutt his number two. Frank was a plump, ruddy and rural type who hailed from the Rothschild country between Tring and Aylesbury. He wrote the most perfectly formed and easily legible hand that I have ever seen and later exhibited unsuspected shrewdness and total ungullibility when it fell to him to investigate the credit-worthiness of would-be clients. After retirement he returned to the soil from which he sprang and brought a breath of country air into the City whenever he dropped in to visit us in his thick and shaggy tweeds.

John was an Anglo-Canadian, a big man with the rugged face of a boxer who one felt should also have been doing an outdoor job. He had been a naval telegraphist and was an artist with a morse code transmitting key which he still used to tap out certain messages with marvellous rapidity.

We sat in our little corner, happily at flat-topped, not sloping, desks, surrounded by racks of code-books, pads of cable forms and including among our equipment a battered but serviceable typewriter on which I became adept with two fingers, and a private switchboard on which we could plug in direct to the cable companies. Coding produced unpronounceable groups of letters which had to be read out singly to the operators at the other end and I soon found myself rattling out A apple, B brother, C charlie, like a professional.

A cable to Scandinavia was always especially welcome to me as the Great Northern Telegraph Company employed at that time on their switchboard a young woman with the sexiest voice I had ever heard. It was thrilling to listen to her reading back my dictation and throughout my time in the department I carried on an innocent verbal flirtation with her. However, I never attempted to meet her, more from timidity than from any feeling that such an assignation would be unbecoming and probably also disappointing.

The near-by foreign exchange dealers were good customers of the department and we were able when necessary to give them a sensationally quick service. The first time one of them shot out of the door and threw a scribbled form at me saying 'Urgent rate, please,' I thought he was using a special private code.

The message was addressed to ROTHACCEPT NYK, which was the two-way telegraphic address used for cables between NMR and the old International Acceptance Bank in New York, an ancestor of the present Chase Manhattan Bank. It read something like

SELSIXHUN THODOLWED

followed by a figure and it meant, naturally, that we were offering to sell six hundred thousand dollars against payment in sterling for delivery next Wednesday. Urgent rate was expensive, of course, but from the moment one plugged in to Western Union or the Commercial Cable Co. a reply could come back from our American friends within two minutes. The deal was done and the Cable Department's part in it finished for the moment, although later we had to write up our records and make sure when the cable company's bill came in at the end of the month that the right account was debited with the cost.

More complicated transactions required longer cables and when really big foreign operations were in hand many long and late hours had to be spent coping with messages of hundreds or even thousands of words, sending them *en clair* when we could but inevitably having to insert code groups here and there for the sake of secrecy. It was all, in a strange sort of way, rather exciting but after a year of it I was ready for a change. They moved me into the Foreign Exchange Department—not indeed as a dealer, for this was an activity in which the absence of experience, skill and a natural aptitude could quickly and easily lose money, but as an assistant in the section of it known as 'Instructions'.

Before we enter this mysterious new theatre and leave the General Office for good, mention must be made of other departments in that noisy cockpit. One in which I did duty occasionally and temporarily was that of the cashiers. This was, and still is, one which always had plenty of work to do on Saturday mornings, when others had none. In order to give the cashiers some Saturdays off like everybody else they were assisted on that day by a junior from another department. Not a vast amount of cash was held by the Chief Cashier, although his bundles of the large, crisp, white high-value notes were fascinating to an impecunious clerk who had never seen such an accumulation of spending power in one place at one time. More interesting was the volume of money represented by cheques and bankers' drafts which was handled by the department. There was usually a flurry just before the close of business —three o'clock on ordinary week-days and noon on Saturdays —to get all payments paid in to our clearing bank round the corner, to balance the cash book and to ascertain how much should be lent to or drawn from the money market.

This last job was the responsibility of Colonel Scott, an awe-inspiring but kindly old gentleman who sat at an adjacent desk. He appeared to spend much time gossiping with the elegant and distinguished representatives of the discount houses who, still almost invariably top-hatted, spent their short day walking round the City from bank to bank before catching their mid-afternoon train to Ascot or Sunningdale. How many trans-actions were actually consummated in the course of these perambulations I don't know; it always seemed to me that most of the business was done on the telephone between two-thirty and three o'clock. But let us live and let live not uncharitably; the system provided a pleasant occupation for some nice men, and no doubt their conversations all over the City and the views they heard expressed enabled them to feel the financial pulse of the country and give sound advice to their boards.

In the Cashiers' Department Pluggy Roche was my chief mentor. He was a little man with a face like a walnut, friendly as they all were and a fount of stories. He was a clever conjuror and ventriloquist, a member of the Magic Circle and a wizard with all things mechanical. He had acquired his nickname as one of the first clerks to become motorized. His first vehicle was a three-wheeled one, having a wicker seat in front for his passenger and a bicycle-type saddle for himself behind. His wife was quite safe in front, he said, because the machine was incapable of going fast enough to overtake anything. It was really a pity that none of the varied skills he commanded had much relation to banking. I remember him with affection, and he was perhaps a good instructor for the young since he knew from long experience exactly and precisely what had to be done, which figures should be entered on which side of which ledger and where each book must be placed when not in use. Although he knew how and what, he rarely knew why, so that there was little risk of temporary assistants' being confused by more explanation than was immediately necessary.

Pluggy enjoyed, I was told, the rare distinction of having been more than once slightly sacked by Alfred—slightly, not seriously, because on each occasion he had been advised by Callon or Nauheim to lie low for a week or two and keep out of Alfred's way and had surfaced safely when the incident was forgotten. One suspects that Alfred in fact knew very well what was going on and that this was his amiable method of chastising a wrong-doer without leaving permanent scars. Pluggy lighted his house by means of a home-made electrical generator powered by a gas-engine and once, when some special illumination was required for the conservatory at Alfred's own house in Hamilton Place, Pluggy, on the advice of the clerk of the works, was sent for. Although at the time he had officially been dismissed he went and did the job. Alfred saw him at the house, thanked him, gave him £20 to buy himself a good lunch and said he looked forward to seeing him at New Court the next day.

What Pluggy did or failed to do to earn the sack does not matter very much, since the consequences were not serious. One of his alleged crimes was to go round to our clearing bank to pay in unaccompanied by an 'outside' man. It was an inflexible rule that a cashier on this errand must always collect one of these tough and resourceful characters before passing under the archway and allow him to march alongside to No. 1 Lombard Street carrying the black leather bag. It was an expedition which I quite enjoyed and the larger the sum represented by all those pieces of paper the more important I felt.

Callon, the Chief Cashier, the only man in the office to whom Theo Jones was less than kind, was called 'Jemima' because of his nervous and old-maidish manner, but in fact he was a very sick man during his last years. I always felt sympathetic when I saw him rush back to the department after he had left and rattle the lid of the cash-box to make sure it was properly locked. He surprised us all later when one of the prettiest girls who ever came to work temporarily at New Court between school and marriage turned out to be Jemima's daughter.

The Bullion Department was another which contrived to get its work done in the hurly-burly of the General Office. Their location always seemed to me the unhappiest of all, for their row of desks did not even have a partition to separate it from the lateral gangway and it was somewhat of a mystery how they got through their work with the constant *va-et-vient* behind them. However, it was no doubt convenient for Clem Cooper, the head of the department, to sit only a stride from the door of The Room in the days when the Hon. Charles Rothschild was running the Royal Mint Refinery. Of all the firm's activities refining and dealing in gold and other precious metals were perhaps the most glamorous and interesting to the outside world and, since I never had any personal experience of them although the gold-bugs sat only a few feet away from me, to me too. Herbert Elton, another man who started his career in the D.O. and eventually became Chief Cashier, was one of them. He remembers the time when the bullion van which carried gold bars between New Court and the Refinery was horse-drawn; it had skids fitted under the iron tyres ever since the day when it ran down the slope under the archway and penetrated Fuller's shop opposite.

Elton was concerned with such routine chores as the shipping and insurance of gold to New York, when the railway company would take the consignment to Waterloo Station in an open lorry with no more protection than was afforded by a single unarmed policeman and a tarpaulin thrown over the boxes. But he did get away sometimes from the world of paper and abstractions into the glittering presence of the metal itself and his great joy was to visit the Refinery in Royal Mint Street near the Tower of London.

People always found it puzzling that an institution called the Royal Mint Refinery should be privately owned. Until 1852 private contractors were actually allowed on the premises of the Royal Mint to melt and refine gold and silver on their own as well as on Government account. A Royal Commission then reported strongly in favour of the abolition of this curious survival, deeming it entirely wrong that private enterprise should be entrenched in one of the most important fields of Government. Under a Treasury minute dated 3 February 1852 Sir Anthony de Rothschild, the first baronet and a son of NM, acquired the lease of the Royal Mint Refinery from the Master of the Mint and although it retained its name it ceased to have any connection with the Royal Mint except to the extent that it received gold and silver from the Mint for refining.

To bring this part of the story up to date it should be recorded that the Royal Mint Refinery remained a wholly-owned subsidiary of NMR until 1967, when it was acquired from the firm by Engelhard Industries Ltd. Although this ended a long association it did not mean that NMR ceased to be concerned with gold, for the firm's position as members of the London gold market continued unaltered and the firm retained their business of melters and assayers of gold and silver and dealers in precious metals (as distinct from refining and manufacturing).

In its hey-day the Refinery used to refine a large proportion of the production of the South and West African gold mines, using in the main the chlorine process. It was originally staffed by Frenchmen from Normandy who were adept at this work and between the wars the French element—chemists, workmen and clerks—was still so large that wine for them was imported in barrels from Bordeaux and bottled at the Refinery. To Elton, half French himself, it was always fascinating to enter this little Gallic world, to see the men in the silver section wearing clogs because of the acid and to observe the expertise with which gold and silver were refined and cast into bars.

He remembers the exciting time in the early twenties when the Chinese Government decided to encash their vast stocks of silver sycee and Maria Theresa dollars. Sycee were silver ingots weighing about a pound which were cast into shoe-like form and, like the coins, had to be melted down and re-cast into bars acceptable to the London market. Shiploads of both, packed in wooden boxes, arrived at London Docks and were transported to the Refinery in huge articulated meat lorries. Royal Mint Street became jammed with these monsters waiting to get into the yards and the police demanded that emergency methods be employed to clear them.

Sent down from the Bullion Department at New Court to cope, Elton organized gangs of casual dock labour to unload, break open the boxes, weigh the contents roughly and wheel them in great tubs to the furnaces. The staff of the Refinery were themselves working three eight-hour shifts a day, seven days a week, and Buess, the manager, was indignant when he found that the casuals under Elton's direction were being given a ten-minute break for a rest and a smoke in every hour. But the arrangement worked well and in addition to getting the job done it was rewarding to see how men suffering from the effects of the depression improved in health and appearance as a result of the good pay they were getting. Elton got to know some of them well enough to feel real affection for them and to hear something of their home lives, and it was a further pleasure for him when he was invited by the firm to make recommendations for permanent employment at the Refinery.

By a circuitous route we have now arrived at long last at the Foreign Exchange Department. Here I was to spend a year not only interesting and enjoyable in itself but also noteworthy as marking an important stage in my career. This was because it brought me to the notice of two men who in different ways were able to give me a push in the right direction. Percy Wingate, a dark Celtic-looking man with a craggy, humorous face and jutting nose, was the head of the department and chief dealer, known to the Foreign Exchange market as 'the Great White Kaffir'. He was renowned for speaking his mind in a forthright manner and never hesitated to call a man a bloody fool if that was what he thought, always adding, however, the words: 'if you don't mind my saying so'. He had a ready laugh, a quick wit and a tongue which, though it might strain to the point of unintelligibility, could never quite keep pace with his thoughts. At his home in Purley, where he lived with his wife, two daughters and a mastiff the size of a pony, and to which I was often invited to play tennis, he verbally excoriated his dependants in much the same way as he did his staff and anybody else at New Court whose foolishness he suffered not gladly. In both places the treatment served only to increase, where possible, the affection in which he was held.

Percy Wingate's father had been at New Court, and so had the father of Sidney Williams. Both had disappeared before I arrived. Lionel Stewart, who was head of the Dividend Office, told me that shortly after he came to New Court he had seen Percy's father walking with great dignity and solemnity under the archway and had asked who he was. 'Ah,' replied the man at the gate, 'that is old Mr Wingate, a highly respected gentleman. He has a room up there at the top of the house. And nobody,' he added, lowering his voice confidentially, 'nobody knows what he does.'

Sidney Williams was number two in the department and the other main foreign exchange expert. His father's job was no mystery; he had been head of the Strong Room for many years. The Williamses, indeed, were one of the outstanding New Court families. Sidney's father was not the first, his brother Teddy was there in my early days, his son Roland soon arrived. In fact Roland, who was to become general manager and later a partner, was the fourth or fifth generation of his family to serve NMR.

While Percy concentrated in the main on dollars and the more active European currencies, Sidney's speciality was what were called the 'exotics'—yen, rupees, taels and others even more outlandish—in which he dealt with an awesome ease and familiarity. In their skill as cambists the two were similar, but in other respects they were very different and their relationship, smooth enough on the surface, seemed to me to fall short of sympathetic warmth. Sidney was, humanly speaking, rather reserved and egocentric; he was generous to his juniors without loving them. He had a low capacity for any kind of pleasure which smacked of self-indulgence, a trait which I recognized from having encountered it in my own father and was perhaps similarly inherited from puritan forbears. His sense of humour was highly individual and sometimes, when the foreign exchange brokers were the butt of it, spiced with a pinch of malice which made its exercise highly enjoyable to the department. From time to time he had 'crazes'—to call the pastimes he took up 'hobbies' would quite fail to convey the extent of his absorption in them and the single-minded intensity with which he sought to perfect himself in them. One pursuit, for example, into which he threw himself heart and soul was ballroom dancing and during this period he kept a pair of dancing-shoes in a cupboard in the department so that he could practise a few steps at quiet moments. These obsessions naturally attracted the attention of the practical jokers and Sidney was not much amused when he was obliged to paddle home one night in the rain in his pumps because somebody had hidden his outdoor shoes.

He had an attractive house and garden at Chipstead not far from my own home and he too invited me to play tennis with him—always singles—a game which he took up less because he enjoyed it than because he felt that the exercise was beneficial. He was not so good at it as Percy was and being barely half his age I generally just managed to beat him. After a glass of cider, the only sort of drink, apart from an occasional glass of wine, that he ever indulged in, he would sit down at the piano. Like his son he was a competent pianist and in this he far excelled my own earnest but unpleasant strumming.

The greatest joy, however, which I derived from my friendship with Sidney Williams was to be invited to spend week-ends afloat with him. A little earlier, before I met him, he had gone through a period of poor health and it was on the advice of his doctor that he had bought a boat. The object was, of course, to get him out as much as possible into fresh air and sunshine and the doctor evidently knew his patient's character well for he realized that Sidney must have something positive to do. To advise him just to be in the open, simply to lie in the sun, would have been useless; inaction and contemplation were unnatural and intolerable to him.

His first craft was a small motor-cruiser called *Victory*; half-decked, with one cabin forward which was both saloon and sleeping quarters. In it he taught himself the rudiments of power-boat handling and learned his way about Christchurch Harbour and the Solent. I spent several happy week-ends aboard her, but Sidney was already contemplating changing her for something larger, more comfortable and more suitable for the longer voyages which he was keen to undertake. It was in *Sirius*, her successor, built for him to his own specifications by Elkins of Christchurch, that I began really to enjoy cruising to the full and to become a fairly reliable hand rather than just a passenger. But all that came later.

The Foreign Exchange Department had a window on to St Swithin's Lane but it admitted little light for right in front of it were the three dealers' switchboards with their private telephone lines to the brokers' offices. On the left as you entered the room was the table at which sat the clerks who constituted the instructions section. In the left-hand wall was the fireplace and on a shelf fixed to the right-hand wall stood the Madas calculating machine. By comparison with its modern descendants this unwieldy monster was enormous in size and hideously noisy in operation. When the carriage was extended it must have been nearly three feet long; its electric motor sometimes broke down and a certain amount of strength was then needed to turn its handle. But it did the job; to me it was a scientific marvel and I often thought pityingly of the plight of our predecessors who, when they had to divide one six- or seven-figure number by another six- or seven-figure number, were obliged to take a large sheet of paper, a sharp pencil and plenty of time.

The machine knew not fractions, neither was it acquainted with shillings and pence; everything was done by decimals. Clearly one of the first things I had to do was to teach myself to convert decimals of a pound into shillings and pence and vice versa, not just roughly but exactly. Two and fivepence is roughly £0·120, but that was not near enough; for our purposes I had to know that it was £0·12083 with the figure 3 recurring as many times as necessary for absolute accuracy. The ability to do this sort of thing instantaneously, almost without thinking, once having been acquired, was never lost; it was to prove of lasting value throughout my whole career and will doubtless stand me in good stead when this country changes to a decimal currency.

Fractions, too, had to be decimalized for it was in fractions that foreign currencies were quoted. Eighths were all right and sixteenths I could generally remember, but when it came to the decimal equivalents of the thirty-seconds and even sixty-fourths in which the dealers sometimes dealt I was not ashamed to use the crib pasted to the wall above the Madas.

My first task in the morning was to plug in to the appropriate brokers and ascertain the opening quotations for a dozen major currencies, which were then entered in a book of permanent record. The same information was noted on two forms, one for each partner, who also had to know our oversold and overbought position in each case, that is to say the extent to which we were short or long of each currency. I then took the forms into The Room and laid one reverently on each partner's desk. Smoking was not allowed in the General Office until three o'clock but in other rooms we could, if we wanted to, smoke all day long; the first time I went into The Room with the daily forms I was puffing a pipe and was gently reproved by Ruddle, who pointed out that Mr Anthony, a non-smoker and usually the first to arrive, might not be pleased to sniff even the fragrance of John Brumfit's Kenmore in the air. The point was well taken; no doubt his brother would turn up later smoking a cigar, but it seemed reasonable to allow the junior partner at least the early part of the day in an unpolluted atmosphere.

In our mail would be brokers' contracts to be checked, confirmations from principals of the previous day's transactions and orders from clients. The dealers arrived, plugged in to their switchboards and exchanged chit-chat with the brokers. Dealing began. Each transaction was recorded by the dealer in pencil, often quite legibly, on a dealing-sheet with a carbon copy which was perforated in horizontal strips so that the instructions clerks could tear off a piece at a time without waiting for the whole sheet to be filled. The main part of our work consisted in calculating sterling equivalents and making out bought or sold tickets in sets of three for each deal, an early instance of the manifold system.

It was our responsibility to ensure that effect was given to each bargain entered into orally by a dealer. On his sheet I find it recorded, for example, that one million spot Ruritanian crowns have been sold to the Balkan Commercial Bank, London, at 145$\frac{3}{8}$. Spot means for delivery two days hence. I must arrange, first, that the Bills Receivable Department know that in two days' time NMR should receive from the London office of the Balkan Commercial Bank a cheque or banker's draft for the correct sterling equivalent; secondly, that those concerned with the currency side, which means both the 'nostro' account-keeper and the appropriate correspondent, know that in two days' time one million Ruritanian crowns must be paid by NMR's bankers in Strelsau to those of the B.C.B. By now I have learned that our correspondent in Strelsau is the Bankhaus Sapt. Who is the correspondent there of the B.C.B.? They have a branch in Strelsau but they sometimes use Tarlenheim & Co. I pick up the telephone and soon a harsh squawk announces that Miss Gregory is listening.

'Good morning, Miss Gregory. May I have the B.C.B. please?'

'Who?'

'Balkan Commercial Bank.'

'D'you know their number? I'm too busy to look it up.'

Our senior telephonist was notorious throughout the City for the scratchiness of her voice; the word 'Rothschilds' as she uttered it in response to incoming calls sounded like a very early and worn-out gramophone record. In New Court itself she was known to all as a woman who would do anything for you if you

treated her as a woman and not just as a piece of office equipment but could make life a hell of frustration for anyone who
was brusque and impatient.

I give her the number and am connected with the B.C.B.'s
operator. 'Foreign exchange instructions, please.' And when
they answer: 'Rothschilds here. I sold you . . .' This sort of par-
lance is not natural to me; I use the first person only because I
am fondly aping my colleague sitting opposite, who is a few
years older than I. I am not surprised to be interrupted by
Freddie Crawford, the third dealer. He is known in the market
and in New Court as 'the Admiral' and is a stickler for proper
order and discipline. 'I should say "we" if I were you. Sounds
better.' I accept the deserved rebuke meekly, remember my
place and start again. 'We sold you a million Strelsau value
Friday. Where do you want them?' 'Our office.' 'Right. Sapt
will pay.'

The ticket is made out in triplicate recording the instructions.
Presently the correspondent comes round, tears his copy out of
the book, initials the bottom copy and goes off to send his telegram: 'Rothsapt Strelsau. Value Friday charge our account
and pay one million Balcombank for account of their London
office.' No signature is required since the origin is indicated by
the interchangeable address but to authenticate the instructions
a secret test number known only to them and their opposite
numbers is added by the Cable Department.

The account-keeper comes round and takes his copy so that
he can make his entry and initial the telegram. He is new to
this particular job and presently reappears waving the ticket in
an agitated manner. 'I say, Wingate, you've sold a million
Strelsau to the B.C.B. and there's only a hundred thousand in
the account.' Percy looks up from his dealing board with a
happy smile. 'That's right, and I've just sold another million to
Rassendylls.' 'Well, where are they coming from?' 'Naturally,
they're coming from the forward end of a swap I did three
months ago. The trouble with you, my dear boy, is that you're
not up to your job, if you don't mind my saying so.'

Confirmations of foreign exchange deals were written in

E

manuscript on special forms, blue for purchases and white for sales. A nasty sticky fluid called copying-ink had to be used and after the forms had been signed they were taken into the filing-room next door to us to be copied. This was the room which had been known much earlier as 'Mr Charles's Room'. The hand-press which had been used in those days to copy letters still stood in one corner as an interesting relic of a by-gone age. Now, in addition to shelves of files in current use, the room contained a complicated and sometimes refractory copy-ing machine. A good many letters, as well as forms and *bordereaux* of various kinds, were still being written by hand in copying-ink and of the letters that were typewritten many were done without carbon copies on machines fitted with violet copying ribbon. They were fed one by one into the rollers of the mangle which spewed them out at the other end after bring-ing them into contact with damp tissue paper. If everything had gone according to plan the operator was left with a pile of 'flimsies' neatly sliced off which, after they had been allowed to dry, provided copies which were clear and capable of being easily handled. If not he might find himself with violet hands, an original letter so smudged or creased as to be fit only for the waste-paper basket and a correspondent infuriated by the prospect of having to write it all over again.

Beside the door into the filing-or copying-room a narrow stairway led to a small room above in which the correspondents sat with their typewriters. When I was posted to the Foreign Exchange Department in 1927 a few letters were still being written in manuscript but most were typed either by the male correspondents, who composed as well as wrote them, or by the female secretaries or stenographers whose numbers were begin-ning to increase rapidly. The male correspondents had dwindled to three or four of whom the head was a man of Swiss extrac-tion called Max Aeschlimann. I remember Aeschy as humorous and fundamentally kindly, sometimes impatient and choleric, supremely competent and conscientious and always in a hurry; a man with a high colour which deepened whenever he had to do with people less quick-witted and intelligent than himself.

His English was very good but not so good as to be incapable from time to time of infelicity. He was once heard, for example, saying on the telephone to a woman client who was non-resident for tax purposes but wanted to visit England: 'Yes, Madam, but I must know how long your stays are going to be.' On the other hand we enjoyed his command of the language even more when, as often happened, he waved away a batch of papers that he was unwilling to accept. 'You can just take those away and you know what you can do with them,' he would say with assumed wrath, adding in appropriate cases: 'and don't take the pins out.'

Now in my third year at New Court I was beginning to know my way about the building and to extend my contacts with other departments. There were no rooms directly over the General Office and this meant that the area available for office accommodation on the two upper floors was considerably smaller than on the ground floor. Above The Room, with windows overlooking the courtyard, were three rooms occupied respectively at this period by the Staff Manager and Chief Accountant, the Control Department and the Private Accounts Department. In the first, which was the room in which I was interrogated by Archer, sat also Killick, a gentle soul with a drooping moustache whose signature was always a welcome sight since it appeared on our salary cheques. His particular eccentricity was that he never took a holiday but worked a four-day week and was invariably absent on Wednesdays.

The Control Department had been established some years before following the discovery of a fraud perpetrated by a member of the staff, an unhappy incident which was unique in the firm's history. One of their green-ink boys, Cecil Lovering, we have already met; Mercer, his chief, was also a member of a New Court family. First there was 'Old Mercer', followed in due course by 'Mercer's son'. The next to arrive was 'Mercer's son's brother' and eventually Ernest Mercer, the last of the line, who was known as 'Mercer son's brother's son'. It is strange but true that these cumbersome circumlocutions were actually used by the generation previous to mine, who would no more have thought of using Christian names in the office than Dr Watson of addressing his old friend as Sherlock. Ernest Mercer, my own slightly older contemporary, was 'Ernest' to me before first names were used as commonly as they are now, but that may have been because at the age of eighteen I was in love with his beautiful sister Madge. This well-remembered but innocent and short-lived romance did not, however, progress much beyond the stage of holding hands at the pictures. It was Ernest's and Madge's father, 'Mercer's son's brother', who was head of the Control Department. He was interesting to me not only as a potential father-in-law but also because he was said to have served in sail before the mast at an earlier stage in his career.

The third room was the domain of one of the most august of all the figures of the old school who graced New Court in my youth. This was Wright Price, who had personal charge of the private affairs of the Rothschild family, whom he served with such seemingly irreplaceable discretion, devotion and skill that he was persuaded to remain at his post long after the normal age of retirement. He was a widower and travelled up every day from Brighton, where he maintained with another old gentleman similarly bereft an establishment of great comfort and elegance. It was his custom to invite members of his department to dine with him there from time to time and fascinating were the accounts which they brought back of the sumptuous repasts put before them. With amused but genuine affection they would tell how W.P., on seating himself at the dining-table, would pick up the menu card before him and say with every appearance of eager curiosity: 'Ah, now I wonder what we are going to have this evening,' although his New Court guests could see perfectly well that every item was in his own familiar handwriting.

The traditional loyalty to and admiration for the partners which existed among all ranks amounted in W.P.'s case to a sort of reverence. Just as Sir Walter Scott was said to have pre-served inviolate and unwashed a wineglass from which George IV had drunk at Abbotsford, so there was found in W.P.'s desk after his death an envelope containing pellets and bearing the legend: 'From pheasant shot by Mr Lionel'. But although he may have carried emotions of this sort farther than anyone else they differed only in degree from those generally felt in the old New Court. I shall have failed to convey the feudal atmosphere of the place if I leave the impression that the partners were regarded simply as ordinary human beings whom an accident of birth had placed in control of a great business and thus also of the lives of a number of other human beings. They were a higher order of creation; it was in the nature of things that a young male Rothschild should inherit a partnership in the family business when he attained a suitable age in the same way as he inherited material possessions and it did not enter any-body's head that any other qualification could ever achieve the same result. When I heard in 1926 that Anthony was going to get married I asked Hugh Miller if this was a dynastic marriage, thinking that it was perhaps an alliance 'arranged' by the family for political or business reasons. It did not occur to me that a Rothschild, particularly one who was a partner in the firm, could marry for love like anyone else.

One reason for the mellow good humour which I saw in Price may have been that John Burrell had disappeared from the scene before I arrived. This was Archer's predecessor as Staff Manager and Chief Accountant and a man with whom Price seems to have been constantly at loggerheads. Price kept the firm's stock account but Burrell also kept his own running record of everything that affected profits: at the end of the year a titanic joust always took place between the two of them to see who could be first outside The Room door with the valuations.

When Burrell was appointed Chief Accountant in 1906 he had been given special instructions by the partners to scrutinize every item of expenditure. It is related that when he was examining the kitchen accounts he found a regular weekly order of one fat capon for which nobody could provide an ex-planation. Eventually he discovered that sixty years earlier a member of the family who was then living at New Court had a favourite retriever for which this delicacy had been a weekly treat, and that when the animal died the order had not been cancelled.

Price's boundless respect for those set in authority over us extended to extra-mural powers and long after silk hats had ceased to be generally worn one was kept in his room to be worn by himself or any member of his staff when paying an official visit to the Bank of England. And before I say farewell to the old gentleman I must record that his generosity was not confined to his own department. From the time when he first became aware of me as a person until he left us my name was on his Christmas list and a parcel containing gulls' eggs or a box of Carlsbad plums would appear on my desk before the holiday 'with all good wishes from W.P.'.

By my twenty-first birthday I was beginning to be accepted at New Court. The slightest trace of uppishness would still invite the reminder that I had 'only been here about five minutes' but the tone of voice was without sting. And I was gradually but surely and permanently falling in love with NMR; with the building as I found my way about it, with its inmates as I got to know them and with my job. I enjoyed doing work which I felt I understood, taking pride in accuracy and in consideration of the effect upon others of what I was doing and how I was doing it. Above all I enjoyed the humour and the good humour; it was a happy ship. The only thing that still frightened me was being left alone, as I sometimes was for mercifully short periods, with the dealing boards. I would hear a click, look up and see that one of the monsters had opened a doll's eye and was regarding me with monocular malevolence. I was forced to plug in and listen. If it was just a foreign exchange broker there was nothing much to worry about; one really could not be scared of chaps whom the dealers addressed so disrespectfully and by such rude nicknames; Mr Wingate or Mr Williams or Mr Crawford would be back in a minute. But sometimes it was a trunk call from Amsterdam or Brussels and I would find myself talking to a dealer at a foreign bank who wanted without delay not just a two-way quotation but one at which one was prepared to deal.

In time, however, one learned to cope adequately if not brilliantly even with crises of that kind. Percy Wingate was careful never to absent himself without uttering a few words of instruction or guidance. Happily these were often intelligible. But one of his utterances has been handed down and is now a cherished part of New Court folklore. 'I'm going to lunch,' he announced one day to the room at large, adding as he reached the door: 'leave Monday till Tuesday and keep your eye on the other one.' We looked at each other blankly. Presumably the words meant something and presumably an explanation was sought later and duly provided. But I have quite forgotten what it was and in any case it isn't part of the story.

Chapter 6   **All Experience and No Inhibitions**

Early in January 1930 Percy Wingate suddenly asked me
how old I was and how long I had been with the firm. I was
twenty-one, I told him, and had been there four years. 'Ah,' he
said. 'Well, I think you are going to have the greatest stroke of
luck you ever had in your life. Stand by to go and see Mr
Anthony when he sends for you.'

The summons came within a few minutes. I entered The
Room and stood before Anthony's desk; he invited me to sit
down. Hitherto our encounters had been few and brief. I had
never experienced his wrath, which in some men could induce
nervous prostration; never been addressed as 'my friend',
which to senior members of the staff in constant contact with
him was the unmistakable storm signal. But I had always
found him formidable, aloof and slow to smile, often impatient and irritable. I had at least learned to appreciate his
incisive mind, to understand his donnish and professorial
manner, to be ready with accurate answers to questions that
ought to be within my field of knowledge and to anticipate the
inevitable supplementaries. Now a glimpse was vouchsafed to
me, although naturally I could not have realized it, of that
more genial and relaxed Anthony whom later I was to know
and love, when the years had mellowed him and reduced a little
the immense disparity between our relative positions. He was
looking at me as though he were seeing me for the first time and
recognizing me as a person.

'Palin,' he said without preamble, 'in a few weeks' time Mr Stephany is going to New York and then to Brazil and possibly Chile. We are thinking of sending you with him.'

This was something I had never imagined. Steph had made such a trip and had taken with him my old friend Michael Bucks. But Michael was a few years older than I, a natural merchant banker and already marked out, in a way that was quite obvious even to me, for the top job which he eventually attained. I beamed.

'Thank you very much, sir.'

'You will help him with his cables, coding and so on, and I want you to take notes of all you see and hear. Show them to me when you come back. You will need some tropical clothes—it's very hot in Rio; see Mr Archer about that.'

I thanked him again; he dismissed me with a friendly nod. I walked out, excitement bubbling within me.

Percy Wingate was waiting for me. I was not too dazed to understand that this might well prove to be a turning point in my career and that I had him to thank for it. He brushed aside my attempts to express what I felt about his own part in it and concentrated on pointing out that it was now up to me to demonstrate that the partners had been right in their choice. The others in the department congratulated me. I found it difficult to settle down to work and was sent home early to tell my parents, who were naturally as delighted as I was. I hastened to impart my momentous news to all my relations and friends and refrained only with some difficulty from acquainting total strangers in the train with the fact that they were in the presence of no ordinary suburban commuter.

The ensuing weeks were full of enthralling activity. A man came round from the Cunard office and I was invited to look at a plan of the *Aquitania* and choose my first-class cabin. Steph himself, who often got a bit restless at this time of year, devoted himself with zest to all the arrangements. He helped me to compile a list of the articles I should need, which was approved by Archer. They included some new luggage, to which I proudly affixed glamorous Cunard labels. I bought and studied Hugo's

Portuguese in Three Months Without a Master. The stationery department issued me with letter-paper and pads, my old friends in Cables with a portable typewriter and a copy of the private code-book.

The day before we were due to sail I said my good-byes and spent the night at the Imperial Hotel in Russell Square. Very early the next morning, 19 February 1930, I took a taxi to Waterloo and met Steph, almost unrecognizable in tweeds and a soft felt hat. That evening we sailed for New York.

Samuel Stephany at this time was about fifty, a short, rather plump man, strongly Jewish in appearance, who hid a kindly disposition beneath a well-fitting mask of business-like efficiency and devotion to duty. His wife, whom he adored, called him Sam; in the office he was Steph to his contemporaries and Mr Stephany, naturally, to boys like me. Most people pronounced the name to rhyme with blarney but some emphasized the first syllable and made it a dactyl, like the girl's name. I asked him once which was correct; he replied that he didn't object to either but that in fact the name should rhyme with rainy, a pronunciation which I never heard anybody use. In the office he was always formally dressed in a short black coat and striped trousers. He was occasionally short-tempered but appeared sincerely to believe that nothing could ruffle him. On one occasion Hugh Davies, his number two, remonstrated with him gently after listening to one end of a telephone conversation during which an infuriated Steph had used every sort of vituperative language short of actual four-letter words: Steph, astonished and indignant, had protested that in all his thirty years in the City he had never once been rude to a soul.

His single-minded concentration on business was notorious. Arriving in church one day to attend a colleague's wedding he was heard to remark in a loud whisper to a friend whom he saw as he walked up the aisle: 'Tintos are three eighths to a half.' He himself enjoyed telling of the occasion when a Jewish stockbroker was pulled out of the synagogue on the Day of Atonement to see his clerk, who was waiting in the porch with an urgent message. 'Well,' he said irritably, 'what is it?' 'I thought

you ought to know, sir, De Beers are an eighth to a quarter.'
'Hush, boy,' the broker whispered, 'they're three eighths bid
inside.'

For a man in his position, with his knowledge and experience,
I cannot have been an ideal travelling-companion, but if he
yearned sometimes for someone capable of carrying on an
intelligent conversation about the matters that interested him
he did not show it. He never treated me as his clerk or runner to
fetch and carry for him but introduced me as a friend to fellow-
passengers whom he knew and encouraged me to talk about
matters that interested me. For the first day at sea I was laid
low with sea-sickness; he visited me several times in my cabin
and directed my steward to be unsparing in his attention. Not
that that good man needed any instruction in solicitude; he
plied me with chicken sandwiches and as soon as I had eaten
a few grapes from one bunch he replaced it with a fresh
one.

On the second day, fully recovered, I joined Steph at his
table for two and began to take a whole-hearted delight in the
most luxurious living that a natural sybarite had ever imagined.
A vast menu was produced at lunch more for the purpose of
suggesting dishes to those with limited ideas than to indicate
what was available, for if you fancied something not listed you
had only to ask for it. Although it was February Steph wanted
fresh asparagus; it came. At some point during lunch the chief
steward invited us to consider what we would like for dinner;
for that, while he would be happy to guide you, he produced no
menu at all but merely asked you what you would like to have.
Course by course the meal was planned, the trimmings agreed
upon, the wines chosen; and when at eight o'clock, dinner-
jacketed and with appetites sharpened by sea air, we took our
places, there was our own menu printed for us with our two
names at the foot of the card.

The sea air was not, however, considered by Steph to be
enough for either of us. He played no games except bridge but
was insistent upon daily exercise in the form of walking, and
every morning after breakfast, wearing steamer-caps, we had to

march at least four-and-a-half times round B deck, a distance of one mile. For me deck-tennis was prescribed in addition.

I wondered if it would be possible for me to see the engine-room. Certainly, said Steph; all I had to do was to send down my card with a polite request to the chief engineer. I did so and the same afternoon a member of his staff, impeccably uni-formed, waited upon me and conducted me below. Uncompre-hending but fascinated I was shown the four propeller shafts, the four high- and low-pressure turbines, the twenty-one boilers each with six furnaces. Everything was bright and clean; no dirty sweating stokers but two or three spruce men standing about, cool and comfortable, lighting oil-burners with a taper.

I investigated the resources of the library and the gymnasium, saw two or three films, chatted in French and English, spotted Lord Tennyson, identified and admired Lady Louis Mount-batten. There seemed not to be very many English people among the passengers but a great many French and Americans. The French women were highly decorative but so flat-chested at that period that you could not tell if they were coming or going.

The weather became sunny and warm, the sea calm. Owing to ice, I was told, we were going farther to the south than usual. Every day I noted our progress on the chart in the smoking-room as we surged on, covering in twenty-four hours the dis-tance that the big jets today do in one. As we approached New York we ran into fog, but it lifted before we came in sight of the fabulous city and through the mist I gazed at last upon the towers of Manhattan. No subsequent arrival, by train, by car, by aeroplane or by helicopter, has ever surpassed in excitement this first view that no traveller to the New World ever forgets.

The temperature in the city of extremes on that February day had reached 73°. Even before we docked at 5.30 p.m. warm currents of air were caressing the decks. We went ashore stickily to a scene of apparently uncontrollable uproar and con-fusion. But Steph knew his way around; with incredible rapidity we passed through customs and were whisked in a taxi, with only a few negligible bumps on the way, to the Plaza. In my first letter home from New York I noted that the traffic, whose speed and density were fearsome, was controlled at crossings by red and green lights.

My room at the Plaza, high up overlooking Central Park, had all the luxurious comfort and elegance to which I was now becoming accustomed; and so it should, for it was costing NMR $12 a day or the equivalent then of about £2 8s. od.

The February heat-wave was broken during our first night by a thunderstorm and heavy rain and twenty-four hours later snow was falling in the city.

After breakfast on the first morning I repaired to Steph's room to hear his plans for the day. I took a telephone call for him. 'It's the chief steward of the *Aquitania*,' I told him. 'He says he has managed to get some liquor ashore from the ship and can let us have anything we want cheap.' Steph laughed. 'It's not the chief steward,' he said, 'it's a bootlegger. Tell him we're not interested.'

The rain stopped and we started to walk down Fifth Avenue towards our first appointment in the financial district. Steph had to have his exercise but the distance was too great for us to walk the whole way twice a day and soon I had my first experience of the 'El' and the subway. The old 'El' was novel and interesting, particularly after dark when one could peer into lighted windows on a level with the track, but the subway compared unfavourably with London's Underground.

Our ten days in New York were spent in a round of visits to all the banks whose names had been constantly in my mouth or at the tip of my pen. Every day we walked from one to another along the deep narrow canyons of Wall Street, Pine Street and William Street and were rocketed on high to one palatial suite of offices after another. None of the men we saw worked at ground-level or anywhere near it; in fact I don't remember calling on anybody whose quarters were lower than the fiftieth floor. The higher one went, of course, the better the air and the view. Every day we were entertained with great magnificence in a presidential or vice-presidential lunch-room. I goggled and listened and tried to make mental notes of conversations barely half understood. I enjoyed the luscious oysters but was indignant when roast beef was served in slices half an inch thick. Every evening we were taken out to dinner and to a theatre.

D. H. Lawrence died while we were in New York; I remember talking to Steph at some length about his work. My opinions even on that subject were doubtless jejune but they were listened to with patience and apparent interest and for me it was a rare pleasure to have found one topic about which I knew more than he did.

Steph had to go to Baltimore one day. I elected not to accompany him and instead to spend a few hours on my own. I bought myself a large lunch at the Hotel Astor, now no more, and in the evening dined at a small Italian restaurant with a man who had for a short time been a colleague at New Court before forsaking banking in London for journalism in New York. That dinner was memorable for the discovery that while prohibition was still in force wine could be ordered in a public restaurant and served without fuss, the only concession to appearances being that the bottle stood on the floor against the wall instead of openly on the table.

On 7 March 1930 we embarked in the S.S. *Western World*, a Munson liner, for Rio de Janeiro in the agreeable company of a couple called Page, who had been married only a few days before. Page was travelling to Rio on behalf of his firm, Dillon Read & Co., who were the financial agents of the Brazilian Government in New York as NMR were in London, and the trip was for him a combination of business and honeymoon.

It was a pouring wet evening. Before we sailed I went down to examine the small two-berth cabin in which I was to sleep for the next fortnight and found a young Kentuckian in occupation. Although I had been promised a cabin to myself I made no complaint, since the American was affable and was in any case only going as far as Bermuda. But I did mention the matter to Steph and he to Page, who went into action immediately. Invisible strings were pulled; a message reached the ship from someone in authority and by the time the ship was under way the Kentuckian and his luggage had disappeared. It was another instance of the lordly treatment accorded everywhere to the representatives of NMR.

The ocean was rough for the first two days. I was sea-sick again and so was the bride. I acquired my sea-legs quickly but not quickly enough, for by the time I joined Steph in the dining saloon he had almost finished the immense jar of caviar which had been sent to the ship as a parting gift by one of his New York friends.

After three days we anchored off Bermuda in bright warm sunshine, with the sea like a wet pavement and the ship flying the red ensign at the masthead in recognition of the fact that we were in British waters. Two thirds of our hundred and fifty passengers disembarked.

For the small party remaining the real voyage began. The crew rigged up a small swimming pool and preparations were made for crossing the Equator, which we reached in what the old hands described as typical Equator weather; the waves were beaten flat by a tropical downpour and visibility was reduced to a quarter of a mile. In the evening, to the sound of thunder from the orchestra, Father Neptune appeared in the dining saloon and announced that the time-honoured ceremony of initiation would take place the next day. The names of the neophytes were read out. I looked forward to the morrow with interest, excitement and not a little apprehension.

But alas! everything went wrong. The next morning a further announcement was made to the effect that the ceremony would not take place after all. It seemed that a certain American had put everybody's back up, not least the backs of his compatriots, by the high-handed and dictatorial manner in which as self-appointed Lord High Everything he had taken complete charge of all the arrangements although he had not previously crossed the line himself. All the older men who were invited, or commanded, to officiate had refused to do so. Steph declined to be one of the high priests for the additional reason that he had heard that they themselves were going to be ducked by the neophytes after the initiation. In view of this fiasco it was with a strong feeling of false pretences that I received a handsome certificate, signed by Thos. Simmons, Commander, recording that aboard the good steamship *Western World* on 17 March 1930, Ronald Palin was 'duly initiated into the mysteries of the Order of the Trident, instructed as to the sign of the Dolphin and the password of the Brotherhood of the Nautilus, and is therefore hereby constituted a Sea Urchin with all privileges and emoluments, if any, appertaining thereto'.

But all this was soon forgotten when I began to taste the delights of shipboard flirtation. Among the passengers were two American girls, sisters, who were going to Buenos Aires to see their mother. The older of the two, who was married and had three children, was twenty-eight. The younger was only nineteen but in poise and sophistication—in everything, indeed, except age—was far older than I. Both were extremely attractive. With the ship's chief officer we formed a quartet and until far into the hot tropical night we sat on the boat-deck endlessly talking, under a moon and stars bigger and brighter than I had ever seen in more northern latitudes, with the sea all black and silver below.

To the three Americans my English reserve was ridiculous and unnatural. On literature, art and philosophy I was soon persuaded to talk freely but that was not enough; they delved and probed until the innermost secrets of my heart and mind were dragged out and all their shrinking nakedness examined. The process, at first painful, became delicious.

Even so I must have seemed quite incredibly timid and repressed. Jane, the younger girl, stated at one point that the kind of men she liked were those who were 'all experience and no inhibitions'. I myself at this period of my life could accurately have been described as the exact reverse of her requirements, which makes it understandable that in spite of ideal circumstances the flirtation never progressed beyond the purely verbal.

But this was not at all the impression of a certain young executive of the Electric Bond & Share Corporation of New York, who fancied Jane himself. In Steph's hearing, unfortunately, he seems to have threatened 'that Englishman' with physical violence if he didn't lay off. Steph, at any rate, was alarmed and at the first opportunity summoned me to his cabin. 'I don't know what your intentions are towards that young woman,' he said gravely, 'but I must warn you that if there is anything in the nature of a brawl I shall have to send you home.' The Ebasco man was large and tough and could certainly have knocked my block off if he had wanted to but in fact no untoward incident of any kind marred either the voyage or my career. Before we parted at Rio he shook my hand warmly and begged me to visit him in his office on my next trip to New York.

In the meantime there were other sorts of deck games which I took to with more success. Tournaments were organized. I put my name down for shuffle-board, deck-tennis and putting. Steph was persuaded with the utmost difficulty to enter for the bridge competition, which he won. My own triumph was achieved at a kind of miniature golf played on a long board where the ball had to pass between two wooden discs two inches apart before dropping into the hole. Since the ship was rolling slightly all the time this required the exercise of a nice judgment. When I not only won the competition but defeated in the final the manager of the Buenos Aires office of the Bank of London & South America, a man whom Steph intensely disliked, my youthful indiscretion was forgiven and forgotten and I was fully restored to favour.

On 20 March, at two o'clock in the afternoon, we saw the rocky coast of Brazil but a storm blew up quickly and the mountains were veiled in mist and rain. The sea became very rough and we could not enter the famous harbour of Rio de Janeiro until well after dark. I stood at the rail gazing at the myriad twinkling lights surrounding the vast bay and saying good-byes. Miss Steen came up and I wished her luck. I was bound for a luxurious hotel but this intrepid woman, no longer young, was setting out on a journey of exploration to the unmapped and dangerous interior to study savage tribes and possibly discover the fate of Colonel Fawcett.

We docked at last and Sir Henry Lynch—Sir Lynch to all

Brazilians—came aboard to greet us and ease our passage through the customs. This great character, a member of an old-established Anglo-Brazilian family, was a partner in an import and export business but more importantly for us he was the agent and representative in Brazil of NMR. He was a bachelor, tall, with a complexion which deepened during the years I knew him from pink to purple, fond of good living, and occupying a unique position in Rio, where he was sometimes said to be more the British Ambassador than the British Ambassador was. Knowing and known to everybody who was anybody in governmental, political, financial, commercial and social circles, he always seemed to me supremely well fitted for his job. He had lived for so long in Brazil that he thought like a Brazilian and his letters and reports to New Court often read as though they had been literally translated from the Portuguese. But he was utterly devoted to the interests of NMR, and in the days when financial operations of great magnitude and complexity were constantly being negotiated between the Brazilian Government and ourselves as their financial agents, the value of a man on the spot who always had the ear and the confidence of ministers and senior officials must have been incalculable. The firm had played some part in obtaining a knighthood for him in recognition of his services to the British community in Brazil during the 1914–18 war.

Lynch and Steph greeted each other like the old friends they were; I was introduced and Lynch, beaming and twinkling, welcomed me to his adopted country. My first task on Brazilian soil was to despatch a cable to New Court, a single pre-arranged word sufficing to convey the message that we had arrived safely, that we were well and that our respective homes were to be notified. Immigration and customs formalities, with Lynch at our side, delayed us only a few minutes and very soon we were in his Packard and on our way through the rain to his house on the outskirts of the city. But it was 11 p.m. before we sat down to dinner. Steph would have much preferred to go straight to bed but it seemed churlish to refuse Lynch's pressing invitation to a meal which his domestic staff had been instructed to have ready two or three hours earlier. It was an elaborate affair of several courses, preceded, accompanied or followed by cocktails, sherry, champagne and brandy, all of which Steph coped with manfully and I with youthful resilience. At last we were in the Packard again and at long last, both half asleep and one of us rather tight, we sank exhausted into our beds at the Hotel Gloria.

I awoke to brilliant sunshine and sprang to the window for my first sight of the scenic grandeurs of Rio de Janeiro, which were not disappointing. In 1930 the incomplete giant figure of Christ on the top of the Corcovado was still surrounded by scaffolding; there was only one luxury hotel on the beach at Copacabana; the office of the newspaper *Noite*, downtown, was the only building approaching a skyscraper. The city has changed but the natural beauty of its setting cannot be spoiled. The spectacle is so staggering that nobody on his first visit, whatever its purpose, can think of anything else. Even Lord d'Abernon, who had led an economic mission to Brazil shortly before, was constrained apologetically to begin his report to HMG with a few introductory paragraphs about the absorbing natural beauty of the harbour before getting down to business. My own notes, when they were put into Anthony's hands on our return, quoted the example of the d'Abernon report as an excuse for what may have seemed to the partners a mistaken order of priorities; but if they found in them less than they expected about the coffee crop and the exchange problems of the Banco do Brasil they were understanding enough to express no disappointment.

The Gloria stood on the edge of the bay overlooking the sea. Between our bedrooms we had a corner sitting-room with windows facing in two directions and I stood gazing first from one and then from the other until Steph had to remind me that we were not on holiday and had work to do. Below one window the Avenida Beira Mar ran along the waterside, the two wide traffic lanes divided by a strip of grass and a row of palms. A mile away a line of mountains, dominated by the Sugar Loaf, was broken by a narrow gap which was the mouth of the harbour;

beyond it lay two low islands like green inverted saucers and then the Atlantic. The sea was a deep blue, the vegetation lush green, the houses dazzlingly white. Steph, not wholly unaffected, was more interested in the view from the other window, which looked over the town and the harbour proper, crowded as always with shipping. He never relaxed very easily and his principal pleasure, when we had an hour to spare, was to walk round the docks and look at the ships loading and unloading there, informing himself about the nature and destination or origin of their cargoes.

The drill was, Steph made it plain on that first morning, that we would walk to Lynch's office, a mile or so away. We set out, I carrying the vital code-book, which its compiler, Charlie Wall, a former New Court man, had produced in an awkward elongated shape which prevented it from fitting into my brief-case. It was already very hot and soon both of us, but particularly plump Steph, were sweating freely. After a little while Lynch, sitting cool and comfortable in silk suit and panama hat in the back of the open Packard, caught up with us and offered us a lift, which Steph resolutely declined. We passed the ornate opera-house, which Steph alleged had been built unnecessarily and extravagantly with the proceeds of an early loan raised for Brazil by NMR.

At the office we were handed cold drinks and a batch of cables from New Court, which I proceeded to decode. Lynch and Steph talked, studied the messages, considered replies, made plans, arranged appointments. We lunched at the Gloria, which offered at mid-day a cold buffet of great variety, rested for an hour or two and then prepared in our sitting-room the first of a long series of cables to London. When I had got it ready in code Steph made me decode it back into plain English to ensure accuracy. I grumbled at this, but he insisted. He was always a great one for checking everything. 'Anyone can make a mistake,' he used to say; 'the man who never made a mistake never made anything. But Heaven help the man who misses a mistake when checking.' Another of his well-remembered maxims, where figures were involved, was:

'Never copy a total, always *make* it.' I must add that I quickly came to value Steph's lessons and made constant use of his precepts in later years when it fell to my lot to instruct the young.

We dined again, at an earlier hour and greater leisure, at Lynch's house. Of this small palace, formerly in the possession of a member of the Brazilian royal family, my impression on the night of our arrival was naturally confused. Now, as we walked up the long drive amid the twinkling and dancing fireflies, I was able more fully to appreciate the beauty and elegance with which the great man had surrounded himself. Lamps concealed in the trees shone on the still water of the lake and the storks standing on one leg round its edge. Higher up, just below the white pillared portico of the house, a semi-circular lily pond was backed by a wall of white stone. Frogs were sleeping on the huge fronds of the flowers, whose heavy scent pervaded the whole garden. Above and beyond the house loomed the immense black bulk of the neighbourhood mountain.

Inside I was able to admire not only the appointments and burden of the dinner table but also our host's collection of old English silver, his library of books on Brazil and the engravings which adorned the cool white walls. And this evening he had added the one thing previously lacking, female beauty. I believe other guests had been invited to meet us but the only one I remember was Lynch's niece, real or adopted, Monica Hime. She was eighteen and I could scarcely take my eyes off her dark loveliness the whole evening. Steph affected greater interest in the fact that she was also very rich.

We went to Petropolis to call on the President; to Guaratiba to see a typical little fishing village; and to São Paulo to visit the Banco do Comercio e Industria. To Petropolis, where the President had his summer residence high in the mountains two or three hours' drive from Rio, we ascended several times. It was not considered necessary that I myself should be received by the Head of State but I went along for the ride, which was spectacular when the peaks were not shrouded in mist and, owing to the nonchalant manner in which Lynch's diminutive chauffeur pulled the big car round hairpin bends and skirted precipices, often alarming.

São Paulo was unremarkable except for its enjoyment of the fastest rate of growth, the tallest buildings, the most money, the most intensive industrialization and other superlatives. To these it has since added possession of one of the busiest airports in the world. We went there in a new express train called the *Cruzeiro do Sul*, bravely refusing to be deterred by the advertising brochure which, as a result of some imperfection in the colour printing process, appeared to depict the train blazing fiercely after a hideous accident. Although the city itself was not interesting I persuaded Steph to take time off to visit with me the snake farm at the Butantan Institute, where rattle-snakes and other poisonous reptiles were bred. Here serum was manufactured from their venom and distributed to all parts of the continent in which antidotes were needed. The snakes could be seen and horridly heard in circular corrals surrounded only by shallow ditches and low stone walls over which the gloved and leather-booted attendants carelessly stepped. Their charges were not very friendly but the boots had apparently been so designed as to reach a point on the men's thighs exactly one inch above the maximum height to which a rattle-snake could strike. To display the extraction process a curator would pin one of the creatures to the ground with a forked stick, pick it up with his other hand close behind its head and then squeeze in such a way that it was forced to open its jaws wide and release drops of white venom from its fangs. This spectacle, to me, was more interesting and memorable than any number of coffee or banana plantations, and more exciting than visits to banks and even to a factory where mercerized cotton cloth was manufactured or to another where forest trees were turned into boxes of matches.

It is regrettable that my memory has not retained the smallest vestige of the actual business discussed or consummated during our five weeks' stay in Brazil. No doubt the notes which I promised and duly handed to the partners would have shed some pale light on it but they have not survived, having probably been considered too trivial to be worthy of a place in New Court's permanent archives. But there was certainly a great deal of work. We were kept so busy that Steph's original intention of going on to Argentina and Chile had to be abandoned and twice we had to cancel passages home which had been hopefully booked. Steph could not even spare the time to spend a week-end amid the floral delights of Lynch's *fazenda* at Theresopolis, some distance away in the country. But eventually we sailed for England in the Blue Star liner *Almeda Star* on 22 April.

Settling up, in those happy days before the Exchange Control Act, was simple; we paid the last of many calls on the Banco do Brasil and Steph signed a bill of exchange drawn on NMR in favour of the bank. Wads of notes were handed over and distributed; we packed, said our good-byes and embarked. My luggage included presents of guava jelly and coffee for my family: the tins of guava jelly were much enjoyed at home but the coffee was quite undrinkable owing to my double mistake of having it ground and then packing it in close proximity to my socks. As we stood at the rail dodging the paper streamers and eyeing our fellow passengers we saw an eddy in the dense crowd on the quay. A small man carrying two huge parcels fought his way through to the ship's side and to the accompaniment of shouting and gesticulation was allowed on board. He was an emissary from the cotton cloth factory whose products we had incautiously praised and of which we were now invited to accept samples as a parting gift. Each of us found himself gratefully embracing four bales of assorted shirt material one metre wide and of unguessed-at length. Unhappily, when the parcels were unwrapped, the patterns chosen for us proved to be of a kind that neither of us could wear even on holiday incognito in some distant and unfashionable resort.

It has to be recorded that on the voyage home, otherwise uneventful, I again came within a hair's breadth of causing an international incident. Mrs Stephany met us at Madeira, where we went ashore for a few hours to eat grenadillas, taste the local wine, slide over the cobblestones in an ox-cart and ascend to

Reid's Hotel for lunch. Full of bonhomie and the joys of reunion she and Steph persuaded me to take part in the fancy-dress dance which had been arranged for our last night at sea before reaching Lisbon. After consultation with various co-operative English girls I decided to go as Count Dracula, wearing a black cloak borrowed from one, make-up applied by another and a blood-thirsty expression all my own. When the time came for the award of prizes the contestants were formed into line and walked in procession round the ballroom before the assembled spectators. Immediately in front of me in the parade was an Argentine woman of great dignity and elegance, one of the numerous South Americans on board. As we passed the Captain and the other judges, the thought came to me that it would add artistic verisimilitude if I pounced upon her from behind and bit her in the neck. She screamed and struck at me with her fan; her husband sprang forward, his eyes blazing with Latin fire. Unfortunately they and their indignant compatriots had no notion what sort of character I was trying to impersonate. I did not win a prize.

Chapter 7 **Don't Know What the Place is Coming to**

On 22 March 1843 NMR wrote to the Chancellor of the Exchequer as follows:

Sir,

We take the liberty of addressing you at the request of several of our clerks, who have been engaged in the collection of the Income Tax upon the Foreign Dividends paid by us.

This business having occasioned to them considerable trouble and increased hours of attendance and as we trust that the manner in which it has been managed has met with the approbation of Her Majesty's Government, we shall be glad if you will permit us to retain from the sums thus collected, the usual poundage allowed by the Act of Parliament to Collectors and Assessors in order that we may distribute the same among those clerks in our Establishment by whom the business is transacted as a small remuneration of their extra trouble and attendance.

With the greatest respect,
We have the honour to be
Sir
Your most Obedient Servants
N. M. Rothschild & Sons.

In due course this request was acceded to and on 5 June 1843 the firm wrote to the Commissioners for Special Purposes:

We have been honoured with a communication under date of the 31st ulto. from the Lords Commissioners of Her Majesty's Treasury stating that My Lords have authorized you to allow us to retain three pence in the Pound out of monies collected by us for Income Tax for distribution amongst our clerks for the extra trouble it has occasioned to them, for which in their name we beg to offer you our best thanks.

Shortly after my return from Brazil I was posted to the Dividend Office and instructed to report to Mr Stewart in the Old Room. One of the first routine tasks entrusted to me was the compilation of the annual letter to the Accountant and Comptroller General of the Inland Revenue which stated the amounts of foreign dividends from which tax had been deducted and requested payment of the appropriate poundage. The original arrangement had been somewhat modified by that time and poundage was calculated on the gross taxable dividends instead of on the tax deducted, so that the remuneration was quite properly proportionate to the work involved and did not vary with changes in the standard rate.

While he was teaching me how to make the claim Stewart produced from his desk beautiful hand-written copies of the two letters quoted above: beautiful but not entirely accurate, for I was sorry to see that the former gave the addressee as the Right Honourable Henry Goldburn, whereas, as every schoolboy knows, the Chancellor in 1843 was called Henry Goulburn. It had been decided that these copies should always remain in the personal custody of the head of the D.O. and when many years later I succeeded to that position they were formally handed to me.

Since furthermore I also observed that the last eleven words in the second letter had been underlined by the copyist, there was evidently a regrettable suspicion that unless the head of the D.O. kept the written evidence available for instant production the partners might forget the arrangement and decide one day to pinch the poundage for themselves. Which indeed they eventually did; but since the abrogation took place simultaneously with a generous all-round increase in basic salaries it was not contested.

My transfer was not wholly welcome for I was sorry to leave the familiar cheerful atmosphere of the Foreign Exchange Department for a part of the office which I knew only by its rather peculiar reputation. People said that although the D.O. employed almost half of the entire staff of New Court it nevertheless always called for help whenever it had a new issue on its hands. It included a large number of women, many of whom could be seen at four o'clock in the afternoon filling in time with a bit of knitting before they could decently be sent home. It carried several passengers and since it could always find room for one or two more it was treated as a convenient dumping ground for misfits and rejects. I did not consider that I fell into one of these categories but the deceptive face which my new mistress wore did not cause me to rush into her arms with much pleasure. I had no inkling that a love-affair was starting which would last for thirty years with only a few brief periods of disenchantment.

The business of the D.O. was the issue and service of foreign loans, the second of the two original principal functions of the merchant banks, out of which grew their present furious activity in capital issues of every kind, capital reconstructions, mergers, amalgamations, take-overs *et hoc genus omne*. NM was soon operating in this field on a big scale. Among his other achievements he perfected, if he did not actually invent, the system under which interest on foreign loans raised in London was paid in sterling by means of coupons attached to bonds, which were cut off every half-year as they fell due and presented for payment to the borrower's London paying agents. NMR were the paying agents not only for all the foreign loans issued by the firm but also for many issued elsewhere and for the bearer shares of certain big companies, such as the Royal Dutch Petroleum Company and the Suez Canal Company, on which dividends were paid against presentation of coupons. This was how the D.O. acquired its name.

There was more to all this, of course, than the mere payment of coupons. But it was the handling and processing and recording of these small scraps of paper which occupied most of the time of most of the staff. In great variety they came in over the counter or by post, sometimes singly and sometimes by the sackful, on one day in torrents and on another in trickles; and every one had to be accounted for.

If your business was with the D.O. you entered by the clerks' entrance, turned aside neither to the left into the Old Room nor to the right into the back-hall and found yourself in a lofty and spacious office. On your left the counter ran the whole length to the stone wall at the far end; on your right three tall windows looked on to the churchyard of St Stephen's, Walbrook. This little oasis, which had not been used for burials for more than a century, was planted and maintained as a garden by NMR as it is today. The ancient tombstones lay flat on the ground, or stood vertically against the walls of the surrounding buildings. At the west end the dome of the church showed where Wren had acquired the skill which he later brought to the mightier St Paul's.

The first two guichets in the counter grille were those through which coupons passed; next to them was the cubicle from which cheques were handed out and beyond that the section reserved for drawn and redeemed bonds, which were dealt with in the far corner under the gallery. In the gallery the Coupon Department itself was situated, with windows from which the state of affairs at the counter could be kept under observation. But not all the necessary processes could be carried out in this central position. The Dividend Cash Department, where the cheques were written, the financial records kept and the listing forms filed, was on the first floor; and away up on the second floor were the rooms where the final processes of 'verifying' and 'posting' coupons were carried out. In the posting-room at the top of the house long racks held huge strongly bound books in which were spaces for recording the presentation of every coupon from every bond. It was an elaborate system requiring considerable time and considerable man- or woman power to operate it and constant movement to and from and up and down of baskets of coupons, bundles of forms, cheques, income tax affidavits, returns and miscellaneous paper; a time-and-motion student's nightmare. But it worked, and worked very efficiently. At its peak the volume of coupons handled by NMR was greater than that of any other paying-agent in the world and the world acknowledged our supreme expertise.

Herbert Elton began his career in 1910 in the Coupon Department; so, five years later, did Leo Kelly. When Elton arrived, attired for his work in top hat, morning coat, starched shirt, butterfly collar and white spats over patent leather shoes, the Old Room had not become the headquarters of the D.O., which was run with great ability from a tall desk behind the counter and below the gallery windows by J. W. Noble.

This old man, as an earlier and more distinguished holder of the position to which I myself eventually succeeded, was always of interest to me. I became familiar with his clear and beautiful handwriting in the sinking-fund registers of loans still extant and I had charge of a small tin box still bearing, long after his death, the painted legend: 'Key with J. W. Noble'. He was known as the 'Old 'Un' and his son Percy, who was still around in my time, was called the 'Young Old 'Un'. He is said by those who knew him to have become rather untidy and dishevelled in appearance in his old age and, particularly after lunch, garrulous. But no one has ever questioned the calm and unfussed competence with which he directed in all their phases the new issues which came along in a steady flow.

These issues were of course a good deal less complex in his time, certainly so far as the prospectuses were concerned. It was with nostalgic envy that his successors compared their monstrous multi-paged documents and solid blocks of small print with his short and simple annals, printed with wide spacing on two quarto pages and containing an absolute minimum of information. We almost believed that when the partners had agreed to float a loan for this or that country the 'Old 'Un' simply took the offer for sale of the previous one and altered the amount, the price and the dates.

Moreover he experienced less difficulty than his successors in obtaining help from all parts of New Court and persuading men in other departments to accept registers of applications. They had all learned to expect a handsome present from the firm after each loan and fell over themselves to make such personal contributions to the work as would ensure their being singled out for special consideration. Furthermore members of the staff could claim the one-eighth per cent brokerage paid on allotments to applicants 'introduced' by them, although not all did as well as the man who kept the accounts for certain insurance companies doing business in South America and sometimes pocketed the brokerage on allotments in his special register totalling as much as £50,000.

For the young Elton the Old Room was the place in which these bonuses or 'touchings' were distributed and into which he penetrated for no other purpose. He seems to have attended there with some frequency and success for he was able in the years before World War I to save no less than £400, equal to the total amount of his salary over the period.

On 'Touching Day' the clerks lined up outside the door of the Old Room in alphabetical order and were admitted one by one. These were the only occasions on which Webb-Bowen, later my colleague in Foreign Exchange Instructions, dispensed with the hyphenated surname on which he insisted at all other times and became simply Bowen, no doubt unwilling to run the risk that by the time the Ws were reached the supply of money might have run out.

The faces of the men coming out were eagerly scanned by those awaiting their turn for some indication of the scale of the distribution, which was almost always carried out by Leopold —'Mr Leo'. He would be seated at the centre table, with a carnation or an orchid in his buttonhole, a large white handkerchief tucked loosely between the lapels of his coat and a pile of notes before him. He had a word for everyone. 'Have you been very busy?' 'There has been a lot to do, sir'. £25 or £30 in crisp whites notes were passed across.

The procedure for payment of holiday money was different.

For this one had to make special application to Mr Leo in The Room. 'Ah, yes. Where are you going this year?' 'Grindelwald, sir.' 'That will be a nice holiday. Take this to the cashier.' A debit slip was filled in, initialled and handed over.

And so, after an interval long or short, back to the unending stream of coupons. Elton, with two other men, had to sort, count and list Brazilian and Chilean coupons paid by our Paris House. In time he was able to dispose of five or six thousand a day and put them into neat and accurate packets of one hundred without interrupting the flow of conversation. The man who at the end of the day was found to have done the smallest number had to buy a half-pound box of chocolates from Fuller's across the lane for consumption the next afternoon. Sometimes they were not through until about eight o'clock, when they would all proceed 'up west' and expend four shillings each on dinner and half-a-crown on a seat at the Tivoli Music Hall to see Marie Lloyd or Harry Tate.

In 1914 the gallery in the D.O. was piled with sandbags for the protection of the Bullion Room below, and the Coupon Department which in normal times was situated there had to be moved into the Old Room. In 1917 the first daylight raids began. These were on a small scale, sometimes by only a single plane, and caused little damage but considerable disorganization. Leopold died in May of that year but for the safety of Alfred, who was very nervous, a small private shelter was constructed in a corner of the Drawn Bond Department beneath the sandbagged gallery. It remained in existence until the whole building was demolished in 1962. Enemy planes took half an hour to reach the City after they were spotted crossing the coast and there was thus plenty of time for Lady Carnarvon to get to New Court to comfort Alfred in the event of a serious raid.

Public warning was given by policemen riding through the streets on bicycles blowing their whistles and displaying 'Take Cover' placards on their chests and backs. This, however, was not quite good enough for New Court. The refinery, which was making munitions, was given an independent official warning and it was accordingly arranged that when one was received they would immediately telephone New Court. A special switch was then thrown and warning bells rang throughout the building.

Since the gallery was uninhabitable it was in the Old Room that the young Leo Kelly was plunged into the world of coupons and spent his first five years. On his arrival he was introduced to Stewart, who was then deputy head of the D.O., and to Harry Hargest, the deputy head of the Coupon Department. The reason why the introductions were to the two deputies was not that the heads themselves were too important to bother with such small fry but simply that they were not around at the time. It would perhaps be an exaggeration to say that they only turned up when they felt like it but they were certainly to an extraordinary extent their own masters. Kelly did not meet either until a fortnight later when they put in an appearance for the New Year 'touching'.

Instructed to report at ten o'clock on his first morning Kelly made a point of arriving at 9.45. He had the office entirely to himself and at ten there was still not another soul to be seen. At 10.15 men began to arrive and at 10.30, his usual hour, Hargest appeared. The counter did not open to the public until eleven and there was nothing for Kelly to do until 11.15, when coupons began to be brought in. He was put to work counting and cancelling them.

The two powerful engines for cancelling coupons were bolted to appropriately massive mahogany slabs at the back under the gallery. Each had an iron fly-wheel which when rotated by means of the wooden handle attached caused a vertical steel spear of the diameter of a pencil to descend with enough force to perforate a packet of coupons half an inch thick, leaving a neat round hole in the coupons and depositing the resultant confetti in a receptacle beneath. If I was scared of the numbering machines in Bills Receivable, Kelly must *a fortiori* have been terrified of those cancelling machines. It was only too easy for the careless operator to cancel a finger along with or instead of the coupons; a worse offence still was to perforate coupons in such a way as to obliterate the date, the number or some other piece of essential information.

Hargest, under whose supervision all this took place, had come to New Court as a result of his mother's having been housekeeper to the Earl of Rosebery, who married the daughter of NM's youngest son, Mayer Amschel. He entered as a porter but as a porter of the superior grade designated for clerical work in the archives. His ability quickly earned him clerical status but owing perhaps to his relatively humble beginnings he developed a superior manner which gave offence to some of his contemporaries. Kelly, when he got to know him, found him kind and admired the dedicated efficiency with which he did his job. These were qualities which I too had an opportunity of appreciating for he was head of the Coupon Department when I joined the Dividend Office.

In Kelly's time Hargest, though nominally deputy head, in fact ran the department, for the titular boss, George Littlehales, did not spend much time in the office. He lived at Mersea on the Essex coast and could hardly be expected to come in every day from such a distance. When he did turn up it was usually about noon. He would spend the next hour prodding his men into greater diligence; at one o'clock he went to lunch and at 2.30 he caught his train home from Liverpool Street. He was called 'The Egg' from the shape of his head; his son, who joined the staff later, was at first known as 'The Fresh Egg'. George Little-hales junior was a mainstay of the D.O. until 1945 but as his appearance was more porcine than ovoid he lost his original nickname and was affectionately known to me and all his other colleagues as 'Porky'.

Another elderly man in the department during the First World War was Gibbs, known as 'Old Boney' because of his high cheekbones. He had been at one time head of the depart-ment, a position from which he had been deposed for a reason or reasons never disclosed. His speciality was coupons sent in by post for encashment, a practice which some tiresome bond-holders persisted in, despite official preference for personal pre-sentation, until it was finally killed by the Exchange Control

Act of 1947. He kept a private book in which he recorded the names of those of them with whom for one reason or another he had had trouble, allocating one or more red stars to each according to the degree of turpitude exhibited. One name, Kelly recalls, had five stars against it and a note: 'very wicked woman'.

In those days, before presentation by banks on behalf of their customers had become the rule, many coupons were brought in personally by individual bondholders, for whose convenience a pair of scissors was kept chained to the counter grille so that coupons could be clipped from the coupon sheets on the spot. Gibbs had his own pets among these private presenters, whom none but he was allowed to attend to. When the Coupon Department was in its normal position in the gallery Gibbs could keep the counter under constant observation and run downstairs as soon as one of his personal clientele, which was mainly female, appeared. The transfer of the department to the Old Room, from which the counter could not be seen, put him in a difficulty, but he was able to place his desk near a window so that he could keep an eye on the courtyard and spot them coming in.

Those who laughed contemptuously at Old Boney's antics ceased to do so when, as was reliably reported, not just one but two of his old ladies died leaving him legacies of several thousand pounds as a reward for his solicitude.

On Christmas Eve, 1915, Kelly received his first pay cheque. It was for £5, one month's salary. Since he had only been at New Court for about ten days he thought this generous. But Hargest, on inquiring how much he had received, was surprised and indignant and at once went to consult Stewart, who also interrogated the young man and appeared to take an equally serious view of the matter. All this was rather depressing for Kelly but he had to admit to himself that a month's pay for substantially less than a month's work was hardly justifiable. The reason for the pother was quite different. The staff were paid quarterly and it gradually became clear that in the opinion of the old stagers what ought to have been paid was a full three months' salary. They dispersed gloomily, muttering that they really didn't know what the place was coming to.

Old Noble seems to have taken quite a fancy to Kelly and it was perhaps in a kindly attempt to make up for treatment which he, no less than the others, considered to be not quite up to New Court standards that he formed the habit of stopping for a chat with his newest recruit. He lunched at twelve o'clock and coming back just before two, when the D.O. closed to the public, with his top hat sliding over one eye and his morning coat not wholly free from stains, he would prop himself against the counter, where Kelly was dealing with the last of the day's presenters, and relate for the young man's delectation one or two items from his large stock of stories and verses.

It is to be feared that these were not always of the kind which could suitably be overheard by any member of the public, for one day at this period, in 1916, a new and strange phenomenon occurred which brought every man goggle-eyed to the scene. This was the appearance for the first time of a female clerk bringing in coupons from one of the banks. In the employment of women, as in other matters, NMR led the way. A little while before the firm had agreed to find jobs for the unmarried daughters of one or two rabbis. These women, not because they were Jewish but because they had naturally nimble fingers, were found to be particularly skilled at counting coupons rapidly and accurately. In the course of time it was recognized that no man could match feminine dexterity at this rather fiddling task and since in addition men soon got bored with it and demanded advancement in their careers women ultimately took it over completely. But the first women at New Court were kept in decent seclusion at the top of the house.

For historical reasons, as much as in response to chivalrous instincts, the concern of the partners for the welfare of their staff was shown in special measure to women until such care was made impracticable by their numbers and inappropriate by their emancipation. Until shortly after the First World War the whole staff, still numbering well under a hundred, was given lunch on the premises supplied under contract by Ring

& Brymer. This was the firm responsible for the Lord Mayor's banquets and although the meals served at New Court were doubtless less elaborate they did include, in peace-time, wine and such delicacies as plover's eggs on toast and meringues Chantilly. The arrangement was discontinued about 1920 and thenceforward only a handful of senior heads of departments, whose responsibilities required them to be constantly available, ate lunch at New Court which was cooked and served by our kitchen staff. All the other men were given a pound a week lunch money and went out to one or another of the many City restaurants. But all the women continued to be fed in the dining-room in the basement right up until the demolition of the old building in 1962. By that time the staff had grown to more than three hundred and women comprised about half of the total. Many were young girls and it seems to have been felt that the firm owed it to their parents to see that they had at least one square meal a day and were not tempted to spend the cash on frippery and subsist on a mid-day bath-bun and cup of coffee.

In the old days the girls were on the other hand subjected to a certain amount of well-meant discipline and Katie Solomon, who was in charge of them when I went to the D.O., gave a severe dressing-down to any of her flock whom she caught entering or leaving New Court without hat and gloves.

When Kelly was taken downstairs to lunch on his first day he found himself placed next to Joseph Nauheim, the top man in the office after the partners. Facing him was Carl Nauheim, next to whom were Müller and Scholtz, and at the end of the table sat Schönfelder, whose son I was to know later as Fairfield. Kelly was surprised and gratified by the courtesy and friendliness with which these very senior old gentlemen received the new boy; but what must have been even more astonishing during the war was to hear them speaking German among themselves at the table and muttering *mahlzeit* as they left it. This went on until it was stopped by a man called Henfrey in 1917, when the war was going badly and there was a general outcry against enemy aliens still at large. Henfrey, able to stand it no longer, bore into the dining-room a *Daily Mail* poster bearing the words 'Intern Them All', a message which he reinforced by shouting the words in the hoarse voice of a street-corner news-boy as he marched up and down the room. The loyalty of the German element at New Court was not in doubt but they never spoke their native language there again.

Although for the men top hats and morning coats were standard wear when Elton and Kelly joined, the uniform left room for personal idiosyncrasy. Some men took trouble with their clothes and others did not. The one thing one can be sure of is that then, as now, the appearance of a man was a most unreliable guide to his position and ability. The most beautifully turned-out man I ever knew at New Court, or indeed outside it, was Shirley Snell. He was a man of great charm, a cricketer of repute well known and much loved at Lord's, a ballroom dancer whom Josephine Bradley welcomed as an occasional instructor, and a friend of the poor and needy who did good by stealth. His extremely distinguished appearance earned him mention in newspapers as among the best-dressed men in London. But he was not intellectually gifted and at New Court never attained a position in which any great demands were made on him. His funeral was conducted by Lord Soper, who asked me what exactly his admired friend did at NMR. It was not an easy question to answer. 'He was just a clerk,' I had to say, 'who wrote figures in books.' Perhaps the truth is that, like many others in the City in the days when the gentlemen were at least as numerous as the players, he enjoyed the social life of the office but regarded the work as a necessary evil to be endured for the sake of the money and the leisure which it enabled him to devote to other activities.

For obvious reasons I would hesitate to say that at New Court the distinction of a man's personal appearance was in inverse ratio to the importance of his position, but that was certainly very often the case. No doubt a man who had neither the ability nor the ambition to discharge major responsibilities was able to compensate for his relative insignificance by looking the part which he was unable actually to play, while the one who really counted for something in the organization had other things to occupy his mind than his clothes. Mr Anthony, for example, did not bother much what he looked like; he wore his shirts until they almost fell to pieces and Eve Icely had to implore him to allow her to go out and buy him some new ones. The most disreputable collar I ever saw in my life was round the neck of G. M. Trevelyan, the historian.

The scruffiness of old Noble, who ran the D.O., was in marked contrast to the elegance of one in particular of his juniors, Bill Ely, who in my own time was still a lily and still neither a toiler nor a spinner.

Bill was not called 'Beau', or by any other nickname appropriate to his senatorial head and tall immaculate figure, but 'Roaring Charlie', an appellation of which the origin has now been lost. Visitors who said of him, as one did to Kelly: 'I saw one of your managers coming in at eleven o'clock this morning,' or asked, as another did; 'Which Mr Rothschild is that?' could never quite believe that Bill, like Shirley a man not endowed with a great brain, was a junior clerk then and remained one all his working life. He used to have his thick silky hair, white when I met him, cut at Hope Brothers in Cheapside, where Kelly once found himself in the next chair. Kelly, without turning his head, saw at once in the wall mirror who his neighbour was but the recognition, Kelly being a very new boy, was not mutual. When Bill was ready to go work on every other customer in the shop ceased: one man brushed his coat and another his hat, a third took his money to the cashier and brought back the change, a fourth ran to summon the lift and hold open the gates. Afterwards Kelly's hairdresser apologized for the interruption—'but I must explain, sir, that that was one of the big bugs at Rothschilds.'

My own sartorial apotheosis came many years later, when towards the end of lunch one day in the managers' dining-room I was invited to demonstrate to my colleagues how I tied my tie. It was before I had been converted to bows and the full isosceles triangle of my knot was admired by those who could only produce a scalene travesty or a totally shapeless horror. The waiter was instructed to bring a small looking-glass, which was propped against a decanter. Almost with tears of pride and joy, and feeling that at last my talents had achieved recognition, I showed my friends how, with a tie of sufficient length, the knot which I had evolved with much painstaking experimentation could be built up: large and plump, regular and straight-sided, a delight to the eye and a source of satisfaction and confidence to the wearer.

Chapter 8 Trankas and Trangrams

The first new issues in which I was in any way personally involved were the Chilean six per cent Sterling Loans of 1928 and 1929. Registers of applications were as usual taken by most departments, including the Foreign Exchange, and I was initiated by Freddie Crawford into the mysteries of the allotment letters with which I was later to become so familiar. One application bore the address of Rossall School, Fleetwood, Lancashire. 'Who's this?' they asked me; 'anybody you know?' It was indeed. 'Pippo' Page, my housemaster, was seeking an investment for some of his savings. Sad to say it did not turn out to be a good one, for Chile in common with other countries suspended payments on her external debt in 1931 and poor Pippo suffered a loss which an impecunious retired schoolmaster could ill-afford.

The loans were fun and gave me my first taste of a sort of excitement which in the D.O. I was to experience so often. The late work was no hardship and the suppers laid on downstairs were gay and light-hearted affairs for all concerned except, no doubt, those responsible for the success of the operations. The basement room in which we ate lay beneath The Room and daylight entered it only through narrow slits opening on to the courtyard below the partners' windows. This room was, of course, that in which the whole staff, but now only the women and the senior managers, had formerly, lunched. Tea was also served there for all those who had not achieved the status-symbol of trays in their own room. It was a bare and cheerless apartment, into which it had never been thought necessary to introduce very much in the way of comfort or decoration, but it had a welcoming air when one descended to it, tired and hungry, for a loan supper and the long tables were laid with shining cutlery and glass and the office wits were showing off.

The approaches to the dining-room were irremediably cheerless, not to say squalid, at all times. No matter which staircase one used, one moved towards it along gloomy stone-flagged corridors stacked on both sides with disused furniture, superannuated pieces of office equipment, battered tin boxes and even laundry baskets. These were, of course, parts of the building into which outsiders rarely penetrated and on the then infrequent occasions when a visitor was invited to lunch in order that business could be continued afterwards with a minimum of delay his host's instinct was to lead him blindfold to the table. The butler's sanctum was a cosy and comfortable little oasis in this subterranean region but it was many years before I was invited into it for a drink before lunch or before going home in the evening. Barnaby, the butler in my early days, was to me a rather grand person with whom I naturally had no contact. He left a substantial fortune when he died and his son became senior classics master at Shrewsbury.

When I reported to the Old Room, as instructed, in 1930, wondering what was in store for me but determined to acquit myself well, I little thought that with an interval for hostilities I should be sitting there for the next twenty-six years, first as the raw assistant, then as second in command and finally as Head of the D.O. It was a smaller version of The Room, twenty feet square, with the same glossy yellow oak panelling to two thirds of its height and the same moulded ceiling. It had a door in one corner opening on to the short passage between the back-hall entrance and the D.O. proper, and doors identical in appearance in the other three corners for the sake of symmetry, two false and the third concealing a broom cupboard. A thick Symrna carpet covered the floor. Black marble chimney pieces faced each other on opposite sides with the fireplaces covered in by pierced metal screens through which warm air entered the room. Three tall double-glazed windows looked over the courtyard and against the fourth wall stood a sofa upholstered in dark brown leather so hard and ugly that Madame Récamier would have fainted at the sight of it.

The adornments included a life-sized bust of NM in white marble which stood on the mantelpiece at one end of the room, while over that at the other end the familiar rotund profile of the great man's figure was portrayed on a red silk handkerchief, thirty inches square, of a kind which had been sold in hundreds in the City streets after his death. Below the founder's likeness was the legend: 'Nathan Mayer Rotschild [*sic*] on the London Exchange', and above it the words: 'Died at Frankfort July 28 1836 aged 59 leaving property to the amount of 5,000,000 sterling'. Along the borders of the handkerchief, in French, German and Spanish, as well as English, it was recorded that he was 'equally distinguished for his commercial skill & enterprize & for his charitable & benevolent disposition', while in little circles in the corners appeared the amounts and dates of loans raised by him for France, Belgium, Austria, Holland, Brazils, Russia, Prussia, Naples and West India.

On the mantelpiece below the red handkerchief was a row of reference books which included several sets of actuarial tables by various compilers. These looked very formidable but with their aid, thanks to Stewart's patient tuition, I was able after a while to make calculations involving compound interest, sinking funds and annuities with only a minimal understanding of the underlying mathematical formulae.

Also among the furniture was a manually operated Brunsviga calculating machine, of ancient vintage but impeccable performance. As a result of my foreign exchange training, I soon established such a close and happy relationship with it that it would unhesitatingly and accurately obey my every command. Thirty-five years afterwards, when I had left the D.O., this machine was still fully operational and although it weighed about twenty pounds I preferred to get a porter to stagger up to my room with it whenever I had some laborious arithmetic to do rather than borrow one of the latest electronic types which lay nearer to hand and were small enough to go into an overcoat pocket.

On the west wall of the Old Room hung three brown and faded photographs of New Court as it was in 1860 before it was rebuilt. These were of such unique interest that I found it almost unbearable to watch them growing paler and dimmer year by year. Before the images quite disappeared I was able to persuade the partners to allow me to commission my friend Felix Kelly, the artist, to make pen-and-ink drawings of two of them which not only enabled us to preserve a permanent pictorial record of the old buildings but to do so in a way that transformed rather dreary originals into romantic works of art without any sacrifice of historical accuracy.

On the opposite wall, between two of the windows, was displayed a letter addressed to NM's eldest grandson by the staff. It was beautifully engraved in the copper-plate script used for the best social invitations, mounted and framed. I lived with it for so long that although I made no conscious effort to memorize it and have not read it or even seen it for many years its contents remain fixed in my memory. Dated November 1910 it ran as follows:

Dear Lord Rothschild,

We, the clerks at New Court, would like to take advantage of the opportunity which your 70th birthday affords to give expression to those feelings of loyalty and affection which naturally come uppermost in the mind on an occasion like this.

From the earliest recollections here of even the most senior of us you have, by a constant and quiet consideration which is traditional at New Court, made our work a pleasure, and it is our earnest hope that we may enjoy your kindly rule for many years to come and that to yourself and Lady Rothschild may be granted a long life of happiness together.

And all the signatures followed in alphabetical order, from

Archer on the first foolscap sheet to Ziffer on the second, those of members of the same family showing a strange and for some reason rather touching resemblance to each other—the Howards, the Littlehaleses, the Mercers, the Williamses, the Wingates.

In the middle of the room stood a leather-covered writing-table about eight feet long by five wide. At one side of this, in an armchair upholstered in dark red leather, with his back to the windows, sat Lionel Stewart, the Head of the D.O. At the other side, in a similar armchair, facing him, sat Harry Brooks.

Stewart was an actuary who on his first arrival at New Court from the Alliance Assurance Company had been known as 'the red-headed clerk in the Dividend Office'. Shortly afterwards the old partners, aware that they had an able mathematician on the staff, sent for him and desired him to tell them what was one per cent of a hundred million. One million, said Stewart. But the reaction was immediate. 'Don't guess, boy, go away and work it out.' It was a lesson he never forgot; one should not be too glib.

When I joined him he was about fifty; a bachelor, small, with sandy hair going grey and piercing eyes that twinkled humorously beneath bushy eyebrows. He lived with his sister, likewise unmarried, at Oxshott. Nobody could have wished for a more considerate boss or a more patient teacher. He was the complete master of his job and his only weakness was a highly nervous disposition. This showed itself, as soon as I had been trained to accept responsibility, in his frequently telephoning me at home late at night to ask if I had remembered to do this or that. I am ashamed to say that in my callow and carefree youth I laughed unsympathetically at this behind his back and was inclined to think of him as a fuss-pot who could not forget about the office for a single waking minute. Only when I was in the top position myself and the buck stopped with me did I realize that it was not as easy as I had thought to dismiss the cares of office completely from one's mind as soon as the door of the Old Room closed behind one.

More serious for a man in constant contact with the partners was the fact that he was so easily and for such a long time upset whenever, as he put it, he had his 'head washed' in The Room. When something went wrong and he encountered a reprimand or even a moment's irritation it induced nervous dyspepsia. He came back to the Old Room pale and shaking, lay down on the sofa, refused to go down to lunch and asked the butler to send up a few grapes and a bottle of Malvern water.

In Brooks, his second in command, head-washing produced, so far as outward appearances went, only a period of stony silence followed by laughter and a cut from the joint and two veg. at the White Hart in Cannon Street. He was a very different type of man from his chief, for whom he had great affection and respect: eupeptic and hale, with a strong and rugged face and a bone-crushing handshake. In his younger days he had played soccer for the Civil Service all over Europe. He was fond of riding, took up ski-ing at the age of fifty, played cricket until well into his sixties and never walked at less than five miles an hour. During the 1914–18 war, as a sergeant, he had worked in the City recruiting office under Lionel de Rothschild, who thought so highly of his abilities that he afterwards invited him to join the staff at New Court. Much of Brooks's Civil Service career had been spent in the Stamp Office and his knowledge of the Stamp Act, that most complicated and difficult of all the statutes which plague the City, was one of his most valuable attributes. He lived at Mill Hill with a wife and five children, to whom he always rushed home at the earliest possible moment but not before.

These were the two men who welcomed me at the age of twenty-two into The Old Room, as they soon did also into their homes, and who at once set about teaching me the job as unreservedly and intensively as if they had no doubts about my capacity and were already taking it for granted that I would ultimately succeed them. Their educational method was largely heuristic and like a French railway official responding to inquiries with *regardez l'affiche* they always encouraged me to refer to a contract, a general bond or a trust deed for information.

The pair had had a busy ten years. Foreign loans had followed one another in rapid succession since the peak year of 1922 when five or six issues had been running at the same time. Some had been issued by NMR alone, some in conjunction with other houses: loans for the Chilean Government and for certain Chilean municipalities, for the Brazilian Government and the Brazilian State of São Paulo, for the Kingdom of Hungary (the kingdom without a king) and the Counties of Hungary, for the German Province of Westphalia and a German land mortgage bank, for three French railway companies and for a hydro-electric company in the Austrian Province of Vorarlberg. A stabilization loan for the Kingdom of the Serbs, Croats and Slovenes reached an advanced stage of negotiation but fell through. But the heyday of foreign lending was over: the difficulties which were so soon to cause widespread defaults were already beginning to cast their shadow. In the coming years we were going to be concerned not so much with launching new foreign loans as struggling to keep old ones afloat. The moratorium, the standstill and the funding scheme were to be our distasteful diet. In the meantime we were beginning more and more to turn our attention to the capital market at home.

A man who had an extraordinary power and influence in this field, who was in a position to bring to New Court several successful domestic new issues and whose name is now borne by one of the most thriving and go-ahead merchant banks in the City, was Philip Hill. I remember him as a florid, handsome man of driving energy, who from comparatively obscure beginnings had reached a position in which captains of industry seemed not to make a move without his advice. For several years he and NMR enjoyed an association highly profitable to both. But he was not content to remain for ever an intermediary earning introductory commissions: he wanted to get into merchant banking himself. He allied himself with Higginsons in the firm of Philip Hill, Higginson & Co., which later became Philip Hill, Higginson, Erlangers. The merger with M. Samuel produced the present Hill, Samuel & Co., whose name is seldom absent from the financial press.

It was Philip Hill who brought to NMR the first new issue which was launched by the firm after my installation in the Old Room and which I therefore watched from beginning to end, and perhaps in a small way contributed to, from a seat at head-quarters. Debenture stock for two million pounds of the London & National Property Company was to be purchased by NMR and offered for sale to the public to pay for that 'magnificent shop and office building' in the Strand called Shell-Mex House, built on the site of the old Hotel Cecil.

There was never much doubt about the success of the issue, since the whole or the greater part of the building was to be let to no less a tenant than the Shell Transport and Trading Company, which contracted to pay such a rental as would cover the service of the stock. Nevertheless considerable alarm and anger was caused by the appearance of a well-informed paragraph about it in the *Financial News* a few days before underwriting was completed and the offer was due to be published. Such leaks were dangerous and great care was taken to avoid them; but the risk was always present, since a number of people including compositors and messengers, not to speak of persons in the employ of the bankers, solicitors and accountants, had of necessity to see the documents.

Stephany, who as usual was playing a leading part in the pre-liminary negotiations, demanded blood. 'Ring up the *Financial News*,' he ordered. 'Tell the head man I want to see him.'

The head man was Mr Barrett, the City Editor, a highly respected and distinguished personage, who would be only too delighted to accept our invitation to call at New Court. He came, and was received in the Old Room by Steph, Stewart and Brooks, myself being also present, silent but enthralled. He placed his top hat on the mantelpiece and seated himself at one end of the table. After an exchange of civilities Steph opened the bowling, at first sending down slow balls of a good length which our visitor blocked gracefully. We must realize, he said, that the item was news, interesting news, which it was his paper's business to report. No, he could not possibly disclose its source; it would be entirely contrary to the accepted practice and ethics of journalism to do so. Finally Steph, finding that he could not get the man out by fair means, abandoned the rules and threw the ball at his head. 'Well, if you're just going about picking up rumours in railway lavatories . . .' Barrett rose to his feet, picked up his hat and walked to the door. 'I've been in the City for forty years,' he said, 'and have called upon Messrs Rothschild on many occasions. I never thought the time would come when I should be addressed in such language at New Court. Good day, gentlemen.'

He opened the door and disappeared. After a few seconds of expressionless silence we all burst out laughing, in which a shame-faced Steph joined in. He always found his temper again so quickly that he never admitted having lost it. The lesson I learned was that in any dispute with the newspapers it is always they who have the last word.

The Woolworth offer for sale in the summer of 1931 was also the result of an introduction by Philip Hill. Some of us may have thought that the name of Rothschild was a household word but for every investor great or small who had heard of NMR there were a thousand who knew Woolworths and who fell over themselves to buy shares. Long before the hour at which prospectuses were to be available a queue formed stretching across the courtyard and out into the lane; long before the opening of the lists applications flooded in. But here too, although the success of the issue was a foregone conclusion, we hit a snag. Starting perhaps in a railway lavatory a rumour detrimental to the company began to circulate. On a Saturday morning, after the lists had closed but before the letters of acceptance had been posted, there were unofficial dealings in the as yet unallotted ordinary shares, small numbers of which could have been—and were—bought at eight shillings below the issue price of £2. This alarmed some applicants and on the following Monday, after the basis of allotment had been settled and while the whole staff was busy writing the letters of acceptance, withdrawals began to arrive by hand and by every mail.

As the law then stood, effect had to be given to every one of these which reached the issuing house before letters of allotment or acceptance were posted. It was a real emergency. At a small *ad hoc* council of war in the late afternoon it was decided to close the outer gates at 6 p.m., to work all night and to post the letters before any more withdrawals could be delivered. The butler was ordered to keep his staff on duty so that refreshments could be served at any hour; the staff manager and his assistants went round to all departments warning every available man that his services were required; the policeman at the gate was instructed to intercept anyone who might have slipped through the net and inform him that he must report to the Old Room. Nobody without a cast-iron excuse, nobody who could not satisfy the council that any prior engagement was truly unbreakable, was allowed to go home.

But few indeed were the people who tried to wriggle out. It was an occasion when the New Court team spirit showed itself magnificently. Almost to a man the staff rallied round cheerfully. The telephonists spent a busy hour putting through calls to expectant homes and I heard of only one wife who, informed by her husband that he would be staying at the office all night, rang New Court later to find out if he had been telling her the truth.

Although the number of shares represented by the withdrawals was a tiny fraction of the whole, there were several hundred cases and the trouble they caused was considerable. Every withdrawal had first to be identified and the relevant application located in the registers by means of the alphabetical card-index which was always prepared as an early and vital part of the issue process. In each case the letter of acceptance had to be withdrawn and cancelled, the shares represented by it reallocated and a cheque written for the return of the deposit. The revised totals for each register in which a withdrawal occurred had to be brought to the Old Room, where I sat writing up the master-sheets on which the details of every register were summarized. The summary itself had then to be totalled and agreed, backwards, forwards and sideways, and only when Stewart and Brooks were satisfied that it was dead accurate to the last share and the last penny could work proceed.

All through the night, all over the building, the work went on. After my summary was complete I wandered about, lending a hand where I could and trying to make myself useful. I was excited and happy, feeling no anxiety, but the strain on Stewart, who showed it only too plainly, and on Brooks, who did not, must have been intense. The situation we should be in if we did not get through before the first post in the morning brought a further shoal of withdrawals was too appalling to contemplate. In the small hours I went down to the butler's pantry for a drink and a sandwich; later I took a nap on the sofa in the partner's dining-room. At 7 a.m., in the June sunshine, two men from the post department conveyed sacks containing forty thousand letters of acceptance in two taxis to the G.P.O. Stewart, worn out, went home as soon as it was clear that we had achieved our objective; Brooks, haggard of eye and bristly of chin, telephoned to an anxious Mr Anthony at his home in Hill Street. An hour or so later, as expected, the postman delivered another bag of withdrawals. The satisfaction we felt at being able to ignore them must have been exceeded by that of the belated senders, for the shares opened at a premium and never looked back.

It was over—except, of course, for the monumental task of clearing up. Other departments had finished, so far as Woolworth was concerned, and could get on with their ordinary jobs; not so the D.O. Preparations had to be made to receive the second instalment of the purchase price and on the table in the Old Room there was a horrid basket piled high with miscellaneous queries: hundreds of letters which must be answered but which Stewart and Brooks had not the time and I not the ability and experience to deal with. We were forced to cry for help and it was given to us by A. E. Kimpton, who was invited and agreed to place his great ability temporarily at our disposal.

Kimpton, a great organizer and innovator, described by Elton, who had met him first in 1919 in the Control Department and later became his admiring and trusted assistant in the African Gold Realization Department, as 'progressive to the point of being revolutionary', was just the man we needed. He sat himself down in the Old Room before that formidable basket, called for a stenographer and with me to help by running about and procuring information went through the pile of letters like an armour-piercing bullet. I was at his side when the envelopes were distributed containing the bonus cheques by which the partners showed their appreciation of the staff's labours. The scale was 10 per cent of salaries but something extra was added as a reward for extra effort. Kimpton opened his envelope, smiled and said quietly: 'extraordinary people'. When I opened my own envelope I understood what he meant.

The Secretary of Woolworths at that time was F. J. Pearl and I was present at many meetings with him, with W. L. Stephenson, the Chairman, and with other directors, at their office in New Bond Street. These were interesting for the glimpse they afforded of the remarkably efficient manner in which the company was run. They had the reputation of driving hard but fair bargains with their suppliers, whom they always paid in cash on the nail, and although the business was so vast, with branches in every town of any size throughout the country, their audited accounts were always ready a week or ten days after the close of their financial year.

The prospectus also was interesting. A new issue man today would be struck above all by its old-fashioned brevity, for it said everything necessary on three not very closely printed sheets of paper sixteen inches by ten. And it told a remarkable story. Since its incorporation in 1909 the company had built up assets of over ten million pounds and its turnover and profits in any year had never failed to exceed those of every previous year. Until 1930, the year before the offer for sale, its ordinary capital had been only £500 in one-shilling shares and in that year the dividend paid had been £175 per share, a rate of 350,000 per cent.

In the course of my life I have been much exposed to lawyers of all kinds; to judges a little, to academic lawyers rather more, to barristers a good deal and to solicitors constantly and intensively. I have to admit that on the whole I enjoyed it. Members of the legal profession always show surprise when, my natural reserve dissipated by good food and alcohol, I have confessed to them that I find the company of lawyers agreeable. Laymen, who generally find on the other hand that involvement with lawyers is productive only of grief and expense, are even more astonished to hear of this perversity. A quibble of lawyers can, of course, be more exasperating than an assembly of any other professional men, even accountants; but in ones and twos their quirks and oddities, echoing perhaps something in my own mental make-up, are to me congenial, their use of language instructive and interesting and their habit of mind fascinating. *Palin On Lawyers*, when it is eventually written and published, seems certain to become a standard work and to find a place in every law library.

The first one who endeared himself to me was a City solicitor already in his sixties and eminent in his profession when we met in the Old Room, the principal legal adviser to the Bank of England and on intimate terms with the Governor, and a man whose advice was sought by the highest in the land. This was Sir William Leese, the second baronet and senior partner of the firm then styled Freshfield, Leese & Munns.

A representative of his firm, himself or one of his younger partners, was always called in whenever a financial operation for Hungary was to be undertaken by the D.O. and it was matters Magyar which brought him to the Old Room one day soon after my arrival. Both Stewart and Brooks being temporarily absent, it fell to me to entertain him until their return. My affection for that wise and delightful man was born in those first few minutes of conversation. He listened to my remarks with as much courtesy and attention, and replied to them as seriously and thoughtfully, as if I had been a man of his own age and standing. This behaviour was not only impressive and gratifying in itself but contrasted favourably with that of some other important visitors, whose dignity was so precarious that they had continuously to stand on it lest they should lose it and who could scarcely bring themselves to nod to anyone of lower rank than a partner.

The other legal eagle whom I met in those early days and who in the ensuing years spent so many long and late hours with us that, as he said, his armchair in the Old Room was indelibly stained with his bloody sweat, was Geoffrey Vickers. At about the turn of the century two managing clerks with the well-known solicitors Ashurst, Morris, Crisp & Co. had left that firm to found one of their own, which in the course of time grew into one of the biggest, most successful and most active legal partnerships in the City. Their names were Slaughter and May and although they themselves have long since gone the firm still bears their names, while that of the former is also differently preserved in the telegraphic address 'Trucidator'. The senior partner when I was brought into contact with them was William Egerton Mortimer, a personality well-remembered by me for his forthright manner and his influence on his juniors' epistolary style: S. and M., he insisted when drafts were put before him, are never obliged and very seldom glad. Morty soon retired and for the next few years, whenever a Brazilian or Chilean operation or a domestic issue came up and the services of Slaughter and May were required, Geoffrey Vickers was always the partner we asked for first and generally got.

His reputation preceded him and for my part I had been looking forward to meeting him ever since I heard of the occasion when a sentence in a draft document which he had dictated as 'interest shall be payable at the rate of 6 per cent per annum' came back to him from his secretary reading '. . . at the rate of 6 per cent per anum'. He noted in the margin: 'I've heard of paying through the nose, but never this way.'

Vickers was also distinguished for having won the V.C. at the Hohenzollern Redoubt in 1915, as a captain in the Sherwood Foresters. Commissioned in September 1914, he had been in action right up to the armistice and had twice been severely wounded. Although we became quite intimate neither his exploits during the war nor any aspect of his private life were even passingly referred to at any time in our many conversations.

He was a tall man, fresh-complexioned, with fair hair thinning and going grey, sharing with Stewart a slightly dyspeptic tendency which must have been induced or aggravated by his working life of late hours and skimped meals. He had the most orderly and logical mind that I have ever seen in action and the most astonishing ability to marshal facts and consequential considerations. He it was who advised us on the Shell-Mex House, Woolworth and other new issues. In the course of one it suddenly became apparent that the arrangements ought to include a conversion offer: that is to say that holders of an existing security of the company concerned should be given the opportunity of converting it, if they wished, into the new one which we were to market. Vickers lay back in his chair and thought for a minute with his eyes closed and his finger-tips to his forehead; then he called for a stenographer. The draft conversion offer which he proceeded to dictate, two foolscap pages long, needed almost no alterations.

He also worked with us at this time on an issue of Chilean Treasury Bills which was consummated when the bills themselves, four hundred in number and two million pounds in total amount had to be individually and personally signed on behalf of the Government of the Republic of Chile by the Chilean Ambassador. His Excellency Señor Don Enrique Villegas was not a young man and manual labour of that kind had not been a regular feature of his diplomatic life. I took him up to a quiet room on the first floor, sat him down before the thick bound books of bills and stood by to turn over for him and wield the blotter. He was game to the end but I never saw a more exhausted Ambassador nor a case where the last signature differed so greatly from the first.

The treasury bills, like all the securities we issued, were engraved by Bradbury, Wilkinson & Co. and it was at this time that I began a long friendship with their representative Jack Hales. In appearance he was quite the oddest of all the odd characters among our regular visitors. Surmounting an almost spherical body he had a large egg-shaped head, on which he wore a soft felt hat with no indentation in the crown. His drooping moustache gave him a walrus-like appearance which was added to by a slight malformation of one hand, giving it the awkwardness of a flipper. There was also something slightly wrong with one of his feet, which caused him to waddle rather than walk and list heavily to starboard at every step. Although he was jealous of the high reputation of the company which he had served well all his life he did not conceal his low opinion of all his colleagues from the chairman downwards, who nevertheless remember him only with amused affection. NMR were his pet customers and in no circumstances would he allow any other representative to call at New Court. He knew his job thoroughly and I learned much from him about pigmented interstices and other arcana of security printing.

The operation which brought Geoffrey Vickers and myself most closely together, which took the longest time to complete and which involved for all four of us the hardest work, was the Brazilian Funding Plan of 1931. The quartet in fact became a quintet, for it was then that Vickers began to bring with him to New Court as his assistant a young Yorkshireman with whom I established a warm friendship which has lasted to this day. This was Hilary Scott, one of the ablest lawyers of his own generation as Vickers was of his, whose personality and abilities, extending far beyond purely legal matters, carried him in time to the top of his profession, earning him the presidency of the Law Society and a knighthood.

Vickers also was knighted in 1946, twenty years before his younger colleague, for his work during the second war in the Ministry of Economic Warfare. But even that was a long way off when we all settled down to the six months' hard labour to which we were sentenced by the Brazilian default.

It started in September 1931 when Brazil, in common with other debtor countries, found herself unable to remit the interest and sinking fund moneys payable on 1 October on her external debt. It was a time when the whole world was in a financial mess but personal preoccupation with a number of single trees prevented me from seeing the whole gloomy economic wood, which was in any case too vast and complex for my untrained mind to comprehend. It was my job, a fortnight before interest on any loan became payable, to calculate the

amount due, to see that the money was in our hands and to prepare and publish advertisements informing bondholders that
we were prepared to receive the coupons for payment on the
due-date. When I was unable to carry out these tasks in respect
of the Brazilian coupons payable on 1 October, and by letter
and telephone people began to demand the reason why, that
was all that I could think about. I was as embarrassed and upset
as if I had been personally responsible. I could not walk down
the lane without feeling that I was being pointed at as a welsher.

Long cables were exchanged with Lynch in Rio and many
conferences took place with the Council of Foreign Bondholders. This was my first contact with the Council, a body
with which I was to have much to do throughout my D.O.
career. Its chief executive at this time was Douglas Reid, a man
whom I chiefly remember for his valiant life-long battle on
behalf of holders of bonds of the State of Mississippi which had
been repudiated before the American Civil War. This was a
cause which he knew to be hopeless but would never abandon;
he insisted upon including the United States of America among
the Defaulters in his annual report, to the irritation of his many
American friends, and declared like Mary Tudor and Calais,
that when he died the word Mississippi would be found
engraved on his heart.

In the case of Brazil it was decided at the highest level that
for the third time—the same thing had happened in 1898 and
1914—the external debt in sterling, U.S. dollars and French
francs should be funded: that is to say that instead of receiving
in cash the interest to which they were entitled bondholders
should receive new bonds to an equivalent amount. This was
not the last funding scheme with which I was to be concerned
but it was of a complexity never exceeded since, and for one of a
tender age it was a traumatic experience. Never afterwards was
I able even to hear the words mentioned without a feeling of
nausea and panic.

The arrangements in which we were soon immersed included
no fewer than five general bonds, one each for the five separate
series of funding bonds which it was decided to issue. Late one

night, at an early stage, we grew tired of referring to them in cables by their cumbersome titles and there was instant agreement with Vickers's suggestion that they should all be given short names. A signal was sent to Lynch: henceforth the twenty-year dollar general bond would be called Sam, the twenty-year sterling general bond would be called George, the forty-year sterling general bond would be called John and the twenty-year and forty-year franc general bonds Pierre and Alphonse respectively. Lynch noted this without demur or even comment and Sam, George, John, Pierre and Alphonse the bonds were from that moment.

The dollar loans to be funded were few in number and presented no special difficulty. The American paying agents, Dillon Read & Co., sent over a lawyer called W. W. Dulles who quickly fitted himself into the team and became a friend. The French loans, on the other hand, were in a disordered condition and the presence of Stewart in Paris was needed to help sort them out. He went over carrying little more than a razor and a tooth-brush, intending to stay only two nights; he stayed there for six weeks. Every day he was on the telephone to us with revisions to the documents suggested by the French paying-agents; one such call was timed by me to last two hours and forty minutes and my left ear felt like a bruised cauliflower. Often the line was poor; Dulles behaved as if we were using a voice-pipe which had become choked and could only be cleared by shouting extremely loudly.

We all had other work to attend to and conferences on the funding documents usually did not begin until about tea-time, with or without Slaughter and May. Brooks very sensibly refused either to go without dinner or to dine very late and about seven o'clock would demand that the situation be reviewed. If it was apparent that we had another couple of hours work in front of us he insisted on breaking off for a meal at the Great Eastern Hotel in Liverpool Street. If one hour more would see the end for that day we worked on and dined at Simpson's in the Strand on the way home. Sometimes Brooks, the family man, went straight back to Mill Hill leaving Stewart and me, who lived farther away and had no ties, to dine *à deux*. This suited me rather well, for Stewart, although he was fond of a glass of burgundy, never wanted more than one and always left me to finish the bottle. It seems to me, as I look back on that period, that for six months I only dined with my parents at week-ends; certainly we became such regular and constant patrons of Simpson's that they knew without being told that our favourite wine was their Nuits St Georges and our favourite cigars Henry Clay. My final task, before catching my train, was to deposit revised draft documents, covered all over with my carets and loops and riders, at the printing works of St Clements Press in Portugal Street, where compositors worked all night to have fresh clean proofs on our desks by the time we arrived in the morning.

'What,' Vickers asked in the Old Room one evening, 'is this word "tranche" you foreign bond chaps keep on using?' We told him, but he didn't like it. 'Let's look it up in the dictionary.' I tried to do so. It was not there. But in the place where it would have been I found two other words whose definition I read out: 'trangram', a trumpery gimcrack; 'tranka', a cylindrical wooden box balanced on their feet by jugglers. If they were not what we were looking for they at least gave us a moment's light relief and were perhaps not wholly inapposite to what we were doing.

Six months, almost to the day, from the moment when the gun went off we breasted the tape. It had been a marathon indeed. On a day in March 1932 the documents were signed ceremoniously in The Room by NMR, by the Brazilian Ambassador on behalf of his Government and by Dillon Read's London representative. But not by the French: a signal arrived from Paris to say that Monsieur Couture and Monsieur Vinson would be at New Court at 11 p. m. to sign on behalf of the Banque de Paris et des Pays-Bas. The butler was instructed to place whisky and soda, sandwiches and a box of cigars in the Old Room. The team dined in a mood of triumphant gaiety at the Trocadero and saw a musical called *The Cat and the Fiddle* from a box. After the performance we piled into two taxis and raced back to New Court; the Frenchmen's taxi was at the gate as we turned into the lane. We shook their hands and ushered them into the Old Room; they signed and immediately departed. The ceremony was over in two minutes. They were sorry, they said, but they had to leave first thing in the morning and would go straight to bed. But the rest of us were in no hurry and the whisky and cigars did not go unappreciated.

Chapter 9 **Are You Getting Rattled?**

Lionel de Rothschild was invited one evening to address the City Horticultural Society. The members arranged to catch later trains home to their suburban dormitories and packed themselves into the hall at six o'clock hoping to get from the great gardener some valuable tips on the cultivation of their plots. And there need be no doubt that they did, for Lionel was not just a rich man who could afford to employ the most highly skilled men to win prizes for him at the shows but an acknowledged expert in his own right. One sentence, however, which he introduced into his discourse at an early stage to set the tone must considerably have surprised his audience. 'No garden,' he is reported to have told them, 'however small, should contain less than two acres of rough woodland.'

The remark has always seemed to me too perfect and too much in character to have been invented. Many years later I repeated it to the late Sir Eric Bowater at lunch with him and Lionel's son Eddy at Bowater House. He did not find it funny, or at any rate did not laugh. He, too, was a gardener whose estates might have been measured more appropriately in square miles than in square feet; possibly he was as ignorant as Lionel was or affected to be of the life and circumstances of the average man.

Happening to be in the Bullion Room one day Lionel saw a new canteen of cutlery on the table. 'Hullo, what's that?' Young what's-his-name was getting married, they told him; it was a wedding present from his colleagues. 'Let's have a look,' said Lionel. And when it was opened: 'Well, that's not much good. You could never have more than twelve people to dinner.'

At the end of the protracted negotiations which followed the suspension of payments by the great Austrian bank, the Credit Anstalt, Lionel gave a dinner party for the full international committee. One member of it related with amusement how the butler, after handing round cigars to all except the host, produced a locked cabinet which he carried to Lionel alone. Lionel unlocked it with a key from his watch-chain, took from it a cigar for himself, and relocked it, whereupon the butler bore it away. The fact was that Lionel's doctor, who considered he was smoking too much, had prescribed for him some specially mild cigars which would not have been enjoyed by the rest of the company. The effect upon them of this ritual must have been perfectly clear to their host but it was characteristic of him that he forbore from offering any explanation.

When Alfred died in 1918, still a bachelor, he left his house and grounds at Halton in Buckinghamshire, the scene of much sumptuous Edwardian entertainment, to Lionel, his nephew. Lionel sold them to the Air Ministry, which established there the R.A.F.'s No. 1 School of Technical Training. With the proceeds he bought the estate at Exbury on the Beaulieu River in Hampshire where he planted an arboretum containing a specimen of every tree native to these islands and laid out the vast rhododendron and azalea gardens which in May, when they are at their best, offer one of the most entrancing spectacles to be seen anywhere in the kingdom. The adjacent river, too, provided Lionel with a convenient anchorage for his yachts, *Rhodora* and her larger successor, *Rhodora II*.

When he was in London Lionel lived in Kensington Palace Gardens in a house which is now a part of the Russian Embassy, but he spent every week-end at Exbury, which he deeply loved. Frequently he would drive himself down in an open two-seater Rolls-Royce, and watching his departure on Friday afternoons from a window in the Old Room one could see from the springiness of his step how eager he was to get to his cherished woods and flowers. Although FLY 5 was a small Rolls-Royce it was a big car with a long wheelbase, but Lionel never failed to negotiate the narrow turn from the courtyard into St Swithin's Lane in one go without reversing, something which few professional drivers seemed to be able to do.

The lane was, of course, a one-way street for north-bound traffic only; Lionel's car, however, whether driven by himself or his chauffeur, always used to turn right into it instead of left like everybody else. This was a practice winked at by the City police, with whom the firm traditionally maintained friendly relations. One evening when the chauffeur was pursuing his nefarious way south he inadvisedly touched his horn to clear a passage through the thick stream of home-going pedestrians. An irate citizen complained to the police and a senior officer was sent round to New Court to say, with regret, that this indefensible practice must stop. So anxious was Lionel to retain a convenient privilege that he sent the then secretary of the bank to the Home Office to ask for a special dispensation, but to no avail: they were sorry, but even Rothschilds must abide by the rules. It was a sign of the times.

I had hardly exchanged half a dozen words with Lionel since the day in 1925 when he had offered me a job. When I was transferred to the Old Room and became concerned with matters of pith and moment I began to see more of him, to experience both his affability and his occasional impatience, and to admire the way in which now and then he would interject a comment which showed his extensive knowledge of financial and economic affairs. I learned, too, to recognize his harsh nasal voice on the telephone; this was important, for if there was one thing which irritated the partners more than anything else it was to be asked who was speaking.

Naturally, he did not concern himself with detail, feeling very properly that there was no point in keeping a number of highly trained and expensive dogs and barking oneself. It was his custom, when a new issue or some similar major operation was embarked on, to greet the protagonists—principals, lawyers, accountants—to sit with them and us round the table while preliminaries were discussed and then to leave us to get on with the job without interference until a point arose which required his or his brother's decision or advice.

On one such occasion NMR were acting for Charringtons, the brewers, in their merger with Hoare & Co. Representatives of the parties and their advisers were seated round the table in the conference room on the first floor known at one time as 'Mr Anthony's Room' and at another as 'The Gold-Fixing Room', for it was that in which the London bullion market met at 10.30 every morning to fix the price of gold. A draft prospectus was before us containing such picturesque phrases as 'keeping the mash-tuns full' and numerous references to public houses. Lionel, who had quite possibly never entered a pub in his life, turned to Hoare's auditor, who was sitting next to him. 'Tell me, Mr So-and-so,' he said, 'where are these Hoare houses? Are they in the West End or in the East End?' The accountant replied gravely: 'They're all over London, Mr Rothschild.' Not a single ribald laugh, I am glad to say, broke the silence with which his words were received.

Cecil and John Charrington were running the business at this time. They were charming people and I enjoyed my many visits to the Anchor Brewery in Mile End Road. Following a remark which one of them made one day as we sat round their board-room table, I have always found it difficult to remember that 'E. & O.E.' does not mean 'Etonians and Old Etonians'.

So far as the routine work of the D.O. was concerned there was rarely any need to refer to the partners. It was a rule that every advertisement in the press had to be shown to one of them before it was sent to our agents, Charles Barker & Sons, for publication. Announcements regarding the payment of coupons followed a set form laid down many years before which amused people in other parts of the office who did not appreciate the reasons for some of our seemingly archaic regulations. When Brooks in 1939 was appointed to command the New Court fire-watching squad an announcement modelled on our standard coupon advertisements was drafted by an irreverent wit in the

General Office and exhibited on the notice-board in the lavatory. Fires, it stated, could be accepted only between the hours of eleven and two; they must be presented personally and not through the post; they must be listed on the appropriate form and left for three clear business days for examination.

Lionel, when an advertisement was submitted to him, glanced at it and returned it without a word. Anthony usually inquired, unnecessarily but as a matter of form, if I was satisfied that the funds were in our hands. The junior partner had a habit of asking supplementary questions which it was important to anticipate as far as possible, for the man who had to say 'I don't know' or 'I will go and find out' was made to feel that he was not up to his job. The main thing, as both Stewart and Brooks generously insisted, was that the gentlemen in The Room should get accustomed to my face. My own chiefs scorned the practice of some other heads of departments who would not allow their juniors to have any contact with the partners for fear that their own primacy might be whittled down.

The purchase of bonds for redemption used to take place on one day in each half-year and at one price instead of being spread over several months. On the appointed day one of us rang the principal firm of stockbrokers to ascertain the price at which bonds were to be sold to the sinking fund; this was generally found, for some mysterious reason, to have risen several points above the previously prevailing level. We were then able, knowing the amount of money available, to calculate the quantity of bonds to be bought. While the silk-hatted brokers assembled in the front-hall we placed before the partner concerned a sheet of foolscap showing the target figure. The brokers were then admitted one by one and given buying orders, £5,000 here, £10,000 there, according to the degree of favour which they enjoyed. Anthony would do this all by himself, afterwards sending the sheet back to us with each purchase through each broker recorded. Lionel, on the other hand, liked to have one of us by his side to keep the score. He sat puffing his cigar, his feet encased in the usual peculiar yellow boots which, as he himself said, he did at least keep hidden under the table, and, always in a good humour on these occasions, handed out badinage with each order. It was also the scorer's job to pass across to each man a duplicated slip warning him that the bonds must be delivered cum coupon or the equivalent cash in full without deduction of income tax.

Some loans were redeemable by drawings, which were more fun. Each bond in circulation was represented by a small numbered ticket made of thin cardboard and the tickets were kept in strong leather bags secured by two locks. One key of each bag was kept by NMR and the other by the diplomatic representative in London of the debtor country. When a drawing was to take place I had to write to the Ambassador or Minister concerned, requesting His Excellency to appoint a member of his staff to attend at New Court for the purpose and remind him to bring his key with him. It was the custom to take the victim into The Room before the drawing so that an otherwise rather boring chore could at least include a handshake and a word of greeting from Mr Rothschild. The actual drawing was conducted by a notary, member of a profession which I used to find rather odd by reason of the contrast between the extremely high qualifications required of its practitioners and their rather humdrum duties. The bag having been opened the notary thrust in his hand, stirred the contents thoroughly and drew out the requisite number of tickets, which he then carried back to his office and sorted into numerical order. In the fullness of time he produced an Act, beautifully written by hand on handmade paper, in which it was recorded that he, Notary Public by Royal Authority Duly Admitted and Sworn, did attend at the office of Messrs N. M. Rothschild & Sons where there was produced to him a bag, etc., and that in the presence of, etc., he did duly draw by lot, etc., in witness whereof he set his hand and seal; finishing always with the words *datum ut supra* and an impressive Steinberg signature. The complete list of the distinctive numbers of all the bonds drawn was then published at considerable expense to the debtor in one or more daily newspapers of general circulation in the City of London, as laid down

in the general bond, and the rest was up to the Drawn Bond
Department.

This was a section situated on the ground floor of the D.O.
under the Coupon Department gallery. The intention was,
Stewart told me, that I should do a spell of a few months in each
of these departments as well as the other component parts of the
D.O. He and Brooks were so busy, however, from the moment I
joined them, that they could not spare me and the plan was not
carried out. I was in the D.O. for over thirty years and head of
it for the last thirteen of them without at any time having
worked in any part of it except the headquarters. I acquired a
complete knowledge of the theory of bearer work and the
ramifications of loan service and fiscal agency duties without
any of the practical experience. This was a real handicap, and
if in fact it was more or less satisfactorily overcome this was due
in part to good luck but rather more to the willing co-operation
which I received from departmental heads.

New Court, or at any rate the D.O., was fortunate in having
a number of men who were content to serve for their whole lives
in subordinate positions. They were loyal, hard-working and
competent but they accepted their limits and had no ambition to extend them. Today every clerk carries a partner's
baton in his brief-case; those men did not aspire even to a
manager's responsibility. Yet we could not have got on without
them.

I think, for example, of George Gascoigne Littlehales junior
—'Porky', the erstwhile 'Fresh Egg'. He sat at a desk behind the
counter in the D.O., generally with a woollen scarf round his
neck and a felt hat on his head because of the draught. The
amount of solid slogging work he got through was enormous.
His accuracy with figures was impeccable. 'What you want for
this job,' he would say when faced with a mass of paper, 'is the
Albert Hall and a regiment of soldiers.' Then he got on with it
by himself or with what casual labour he could find. He was
utterly reliable when issues were in progress and he was
impregnably calm amid the bustle. While the experts in the
Old Room were engaged on the tricky job of working out the

scale of allotment he would be outside agreeing the cash. But he would not have changed places with them. He had no ambition at all to run the show himself. He was often mildly critical of what went on in the Old Room and never hesitated to tell us if he thought we were on the wrong tack. But one only had to say: 'Well, Porky, you try it. Come and have a go yourself and see what you can make of it.' At once he would shake his head and say with his own endearing diffidence that he knew perfectly well that such matters were too complicated for him and that he couldn't begin to cope with them.

Porky lived in a converted coastguard's cottage at Hythe in Kent. During the second war he was one of the ageing stalwarts who kept the office running and spent five hours a day travelling in order to do so. He was a tower of strength—a Martello tower, round, rather squat and of old-fashioned construction, well suited to its time and purpose but not strong enough to have survived for long under modern conditions.

Sitting a few feet away from Porky was Percy Wyatt, the wearer of the only surviving beard at New Court. Save that both were members of the D.O. and both bachelors they had nothing in common. While Porky was friendly and humorous and popular, Percy was reserved and self-contained, a man not observed to have any close friends in the office; Porky was unpressed and cardiganed while Percy was neat and dapper, for ever brushing invisible specks from the lapels of his black coat with the backs of his fingers. It was Percy's job to hand out the daily cheques in payment of coupons and drawn bonds against the tickets, rather like cloakroom tickets, which were issued at the time of presentation. He also dealt with the routine letters received in the D.O.; dealt with them that is to say, to the extent that he opened them and recorded them in an expensive book composed of hand-made paper and massively bound. For reply he generally brought them into the Old Room unless they were concerned with one or other of the only two registers of securities, neither of them large or active, which NMR kept in those days.

Percy Wyatt's special peculiarity, however, was his practice of keeping his monthly salary cheques in his desk for half a year or more instead of paying them into his bank, brushing aside complaints with the remark that they were really too small to bother with. He habitually did the same thing with his personal dividend warrants. Company secretaries or registrars some-times came to see him at New Court and implored him almost with tears in their eyes to clear outstanding warrants so that they could close their books. His colleagues who overheard these conversations found them entertaining but they were not amused when, as sometimes happened, they themselves were the victims of the old man's wayward behaviour. It was frequently arranged in connection with a new issue that some kind of temporary document or scrip certificate would be delivered in the first place to successful applicants and these would circulate for an interim period until the definitive security was ready, when they would be brought in and exchanged. The issue could not be tidily completed until all the temporary scrip certificates had been so exchanged. On one occasion a single such certificate remained exasperatingly out-standing for several months despite all efforts to locate it. It was, of course, in bearer form and had changed hands many times, necessitating innumerable telephone calls in the endeavour to trace its passage from one holder to the next. Percy Wyatt, seated in his cubicle, listened to this detective work going on behind him day after day while all the while the missing docu-ment was reposing in his desk.

This sort of thing did not endear him to his colleagues and it was not strange that he had no close friends in the D.O. He was nevertheless a man of considerable experience and ability, a fact recognized by Stewart and Brooks, whose custom it was, when a prospectus was in its final stages, to send the latest proof out to Percy and ask him to cast his eye over it.

He astonished everybody by marrying late in life after his retirement, but nobody was much surprised when, dying a few years later, he was found to have left quite a substantial fortune. He spent a great deal of time in the office dealing with his own investments and **anyone** who showed interest in what he was

up to, rather than idle curiosity, would usually receive ungrudg-
ing advice and the offer: 'Can I get you some?'

Looking back on the early thirties at New Court with older
and more knowledgeable eyes I am struck by the extraordinary
and perhaps somewhat shameful contrast between my own
happiness in those years and the acute anxiety which they
brought to the men who were really running the business. The
Wall Street crash, the financial crisis, the failure of the Credit
Anstalt, the defaults one after another of the debtor countries,
all these formed only the dimly discerned background against
which I was learning the technique of a new job. Discovering
how the D.O. system worked and how its far-flung components
interlocked, poring over general bonds, contracts, agreements
and trust deeds, or simply trying to introduce some order into
the Old Room's chaotic files, I did not pause to wonder where
the firm's profits were coming from or how it was that in those
difficult days nobody, however insignificant his contribution,
was asked to leave or even to accept a reduced salary.

I was dealing with matters of some complexity and I was
beginning to carry the responsibility of planning and directing
the work of others; but the ultimate responsibility was not mine.
If I did not know the answer there were always men above me
whom I could ask. Not yet was I in the lonely and uncomfortable position at the top where, although the partners were
there to take final decisions, I was the man upon whose technical expertise and advice their decisions would have to be based;
where I would be faced with the chill realization that although
I might not know all there was to know about fiscal agency
techniques, nobody in the office knew more.

The absence of dull routine was pleasant. No day was
exactly like another; each brought different problems. I began
to draft letters—to dress some of the firm's shop windows, so to
speak, or to draw some of the faces which it showed to the outside world. Unhappily many of the letters which I was called
upon to write consisted of explanations of the reasons why
coupons which had matured could not in fact be paid and of
attempts to appease the wrath of disappointed investors, letters

upon which I expended much effort in the vain hope that literary elegance might somehow disguise unwelcome contents. But there was also much correspondence of a more rewarding kind with foreign banks on international operations.

When I joined them my two bosses were in the throes of one such operation for Hungary. In anticipation of a long-term loan (which world conditions, as it turned out, rendered impracticable) a line of yearling treasury bills was placed with a number of institutions in London, with tranches in Switzerland and Sweden. Such operations always brought interesting visitors as well as lawyers: that for Hungary brought to the Old Room 'a constant and grateful visitor', as he described himself on the silver ash-tray which he afterwards presented to us, in the shape of Sir William Athelstane Meredith Goode, K.B.E.

From 1923 to 1941 Goode was an official financial adviser to the Hungarian Government, whose confidence he clearly enjoyed. His recreations were given in *Who's Who* as 'fishing, cabling and advising'. I never saw him in action as an angler but I had many opportunities of observing his devotion to the other two activities, the nature of which suggests correctly that there was not a sharp division between his work and his amusements. He had had a varied career. At an early stage in it he had been joint news editor of the *Daily Mail*. He was an expert in communications, in which capacity he had served in World War I in the Ministry of Food and was to do so again in 1941. Between the wars he was a member of various governmental and inter-governmental commissions concerned with food, reparations and relief.

He was an afternoon man. His voice, when he appeared at New Court about tea-time, had the sound of hob-nailed boots treading on loose gravel; but in the morning, as I discovered when for the first and last time I telephoned him before noon, it was so impenetrably hoarse and so continually interrupted by coughing as to render him almost incapable of speaking at all. On arrival in the Old Room he invariably called for a bottle of Malvern water, a lubricant which counteracted to some extent the effect of the Turkish cigarettes which he chain-smoked. If, as usual, he had eaten no lunch he also munched chocolate *langues de chat* which he bought at Prestat's in St Swithin's Lane before settling down to work with us. He reached his best as the day wore on and in the evening, gay and hospitable, gave elaborate and luxurious dinner parties at his house in West-bourne Gardens. Brooks was invited to these and sometimes went when the call of his family was not too strong; Stewart was invited too but did not go. I, very naturally, was not invited but frequently, if I was ready to leave at the same time as himself, Goode stood me a brandy and soda at a neighbouring bar on the way home. With his thick iron-grey hair and square pale face he was a familiar figure at New Court for several years.

Another whom I met at this time and who was around even longer, indeed until the fifties, was Wilhelm Regendanz, banker and Doctor of Law. It was of him I thought with affection when a certain German, an industrialist and entrepreneur with multifarious and widespread interests, was described by another, whose English was not quite perfect, as having 'how do you say? —a finger in every tart'. Dr Regendanz had at one time been general manager of the Credit Anstalt in Vienna. Among other things he owned the Baltic island of Sylt and the railway leading thereto, or at least was the principal shareholder in the company which owned them. He had a magnificent house in Berlin-Dahlem and knew everybody who was anybody in Germany. But they were all, from the point of view of the Nazis, the wrong people. Shortly before the Night of the Long Knives in 1934 he gave a dinner party at his house; after that night, of the twenty men present only he himself and the French Ambassador were left alive. For Regendanz it was a clear and unmistakable red light. He left Germany and settled in England. With his extensive interests he must have been a very rich man. How much of his fortune he succeeded in getting out I did not ask; it was enough, at any rate, for him to buy a large house on the edge of Richmond Park, to educate and settle his children and to live in reasonable comfort.

He it was who introduced to NMR the Austrian hydro-electric company called Vorarlberger Illwerke A. G. at Bregenz which supplied power to the Ruhr and for which the firm in 1929 made an issue of £2,000,000 First Mortgage Sterling Bonds. In spite of all the careful work which went into it and the fundamental soundness of the security, the issue was not enthusiastically received and most of the bonds went to the underwriters. I missed the offer for sale but came in for the inevitable default.

For a number of reasons my memories of V.I.W., as it was called, are among the happiest I have of old New Court. The settlement which we eventually achieved after I had become head of the D.O. was without question the best of any of the pre-war foreign sterling debts. This is something in which I take considerable pride, although much of the credit must go to H. A. Brooks, who laid the foundations but retired before the end. Furthermore it was a team job, and the team was composed of friends who worked very happily together: in addition to myself there were Hilary Scott and his German-speaking colleague, Otto Giesen; Humphrey Rodyk of Royal Exchange Assurance, the trustees of the bonds, who died at a sadly early age; and of course Regendanz himself. The good Doktor worked tirelessly for the settlement of a loan for which he felt himself personally responsible; many were the journeys we made together, the conferences we attended and the bottles of his beloved Rhine wine we drank in pursuance of the goal which we reached before he, too, died. The negotiations lasted several years. Another pleasant feature of them was the lovable personality of Anton Ammann, the managing director of V.I.W., a civil engineer with a wonderful grasp of financial matters and an equally wonderful ability to discuss them in English. Yet another was the delightful surroundings in which our talks took place: the Austrian Government was opposed to Ammann's coming to London and we met in Salzburg, amid the snow-covered mountains of Vorarlberg or in the Hotel Baur au Lac in Zürich, one of the greatest hotels in Europe.

In 1930 the firm still had an agent in Belgrade, who had worked with Stewart and Brooks on the abortive Yugoslavian stabilization loan and whom I was just in time to meet. This was an entertaining character called R. H. Porters. He turned up one day bearing gifts of slivovitz, the famous plum brandy of the country, for which I immediately acquired a liking but happily, since the supply dried up, not an addiction. There was now little or nothing for him to do for NMR in Belgrade; he soon disappeared from the scene to fresh woods and no more heard in the Old Room were his stories of that little-known capital.

Our agent in Chile, David Blair, I did not meet, for he was already advanced in years and did not come to London in my time. But Harry Lynch came breezily in from Brazil, reviving memories of the exciting weeks I had spent there with him. This was an adventurous trip for him: ever ready for new experiences he had flown from Rio to Friedrichshafen in the Graf Zeppelin and thus was full of traveller's tales of more than routine interest.

The firm's principal banking correspondents in Germany, with whom we were closely associated, were M. M. Warburg & Co. of Hamburg. One day one of their young partners arrived at New Court, a dark, handsome man only a few years older than I, for a stay of a week or two during which it was thought useful for him to spend a few days in the D.O. He sat with us in the Old Room and listened to a discourse from my seniors and it then fell to me, on the more practical side, to show him round the departments and explain our elaborate and efficient system. His name was Siegmund Warburg, 'Sigi' to his many friends. I found him friendly, interested and highly intelligent; a man destined to go far, we said to ourselves, although in what direction we could not guess. About this time we received out of the blue a letter inviting us to finance a quartz mine producing the material, so the writer claimed, used for making 'the large crystal balls of the mystics'. Apparatus of that kind would have been extremely useful on the many occasions when we tried to peer into the future: certainly only a large and sensitive crystal ball could have told us then that our young guest from Germany would found in London the famous and successful merchant banking firm of S. G. Warburg & Co. Ltd and achieve a knighthood and a dazzling reputation.

A visitor from nearer home whom I took on a similar tour of the D.O. and to whom I gave a similar commentary without arousing a comparable interest was Victor Rothschild. His uncle, the second Lord Rothschild, died in 1937 and it was just after he succeeded to the title at the age of twenty-six that, still in mourning, he came among us. But his interests were in science, more particularly in biology, and not in finance. Although like his father, Charles, he did concern himself for a time with the gold-refining side of the business he was not seriously tempted to devote his powerful intellect to banking and to take the partnership he could have had.

Shortly after we met he threw himself with all his driving energy into the work of rescuing Jews in Germany, so far as it was possible to do so, from the Nazi holocaust. He needed assistance from New Court and since the D.O. was not at that time particularly hard pressed I was seconded to work with him. The French Room next to the porters' lodge was put at my disposal together with a small squad of girls. This episode was a part of my early career at New Court and must therefore have a place in this narrative but it is one for which the light-hearted tone of the rest of the story will not do. Taking in money and paying it in to the appeal account of the Central British Fund for German Jewry was all right; but there was also correspondence from Germany which it was decided had to be dealt with at New Court and not just passed on to the office of the C.B.F. Day after day letters came in direct from Jews in the heart of the conflagration, letters describing unimaginable sufferings, letters appealing piteously for help. It was my task to read them and to reply to them. I was given guidance, in general, as to what I could say and I dictated my poor answers, knowing that a few brief inadequate lines from an unknown writer in London would represent for the recipients their only hope. 'Are you getting rattled, Palin?' Lord Rothschild asked me at one point. Foolishly and untruly I said I was not. For a moment I really thought he was merely concerned lest I and my few helpers should be overwhelmed by the volume of work.

Chapter 10 **Lead It Fair**

One afternoon in the spring of 1939 Sidney Williams, whose custom it was to take tea in the Bullion Room over which his father had once ruled, looked in on us on his way back to his exotic currencies. Stewart had retired, leaving Brooks in charge and me as his *de facto* if not officially acknowledged second in command. Would I like to spend the four days of the Easter holiday afloat? And would Brooks allow me to leave early on the Thursday and arrive a little later than usual on the following Tuesday morning? The answer was 'yes' to both questions. If either of us reflected that it was going to be our last sailing holiday together the thought was unspoken.

We caught the 4.30 from Waterloo, arriving at Christchurch at dusk. *Sirius* lay at her moorings in the river off Elkins's boat-yard. We rowed out to her in the dinghy, rolled back the canvas cover from the cockpit, started up and cast off. The skipper wanted to be at sea early the next morning, so we sailed across the harbour and anchored near its mouth at Mudeford, where the whole great body of water emptied itself through a fast-running channel only a few yards wide. Sidney cooked chops and potatoes on the primus stove and afterwards produced cigars. Last thing before turning in I went on deck as usual for 'Operation Maypole', which consisted of winding one of the halyards in a tight spiral round the mast to prevent our being kept awake by the slapping of ropes.

Throughout the week-end the weather displayed a strange

symbolic appropriateness. The sun shone from a cloudless sky but from the east the wind blew with an icy and relentless force. Early on Good Friday morning Sidney brought me a cup of tea in my bunk. Again according to the usual procedure I crawled into the tiny forepeak which besides housing the anchor chain contained a wash-basin, there to shave and wash while the skipper did the same in the galley and then cooked bacon and eggs. Before nine o'clock the anchor had been hauled in and made fast and we were heading cautiously down the narrow channel: cautiously, because the entrance was protected by a sand-bar covered by only three or four feet of water and, pounded by the winter's storms, would usually be found to be in a position quite different from that of the previous summer. Sidney felt his way gingerly across. In a few minutes we were pitching in Christchurch Bay and, no longer under the lee of the land, exposed to the full strength of the east wind.

It was bitterly cold. Sidney had scorned any suggestion that the design of *Sirius* should include a glass-enclosed cockpit or even a windscreen. Only when the wind was at our backs could we find any comfort, so we turned west and fled before it. Well out to sea we passed Bournemouth, heading for Sandbanks and Poole. We entered Poole Harbour and sailed across that huge stretch of water, past Brownsea Island, and into the River Frome. At last, when we were some way up the river and almost in sight of Wareham, we began to get out of the wind. We made fast to the bank, secured the canvas cover along the weather side of the cockpit and set a sheer-leg to prevent the boat heeling over when the tide fell and dropped her on to the mud. At last, sitting on the floor, we felt warm in the sun and could take some clothes off.

One summer Sunday afternoon several years earlier, when I was nineteen or twenty, I went for a stroll in a wood near St Albans with a pretty dark girl of about the same age whom I had met there quite by chance. It was warm and the bright sunlight filtered through the trees on to the grass and the wild flowers. Birds were singing. We roamed idly, talking impersonally of this and that, and came presently to a wooden bungalow set in a clearing, where the girl's father and mother were sitting on the veranda, he smoking a pipe and reading, she knitting. I was introduced; they made me welcome and gave me tea. The entire incident was totally unremarkable save for one circumstance: all four of us, all the time, were stark naked.

My experiments with the cult of nudism had begun, out of simple curiosity, when I answered an advertisement for people interested in starting a 'colony', as they used to be called, in Essex near Billericay. I was invited rather surprisingly to a barrister's chambers off Chancery Lane where I met among others W. S. M. Knight, auther of a do-it-yourself book on every-day legal problems. It soon became clear to me that the advertisers were looking for people to invest capital in the enterprise. They had realized from my letter that money was not to be looked for from me, except a modest guinea or two by way of subscription, but they invited me to call as one of the few respondents who had written from home and not from an obvious accommodation address. The proposed purchase of land at Billericay came to nothing but Knight, a highly respectable pioneer, impressed with the sincerity of my interest, put me in touch with an established club in London where I could pursue my researches.

This was at the time when I was in the Foreign Exchange Department and during lulls in the day's work I reported progress to my colleagues, flattered by the attention with which they listened to my tales and not at all disconcerted by their hoots of laughter. It was, naturally enough, the comic side of these activities which struck them most forcibly and certainly nothing could have been more ridiculous than the goings-on in that basement off the King's Road in Chelsea in which my practical experience began. The group met in a single room about twenty-five feet long in which the members met, undressed, chatted, drank coffee and played deck-tennis. The height of absurdity was reached one evening when, having arrived to find nobody there and being about to leave, I met a middle-aged woman coming down the stairs who begged me to stay for a game. We proceeded solemnly to disrobe in our respective corners of the room and then to fling the rubber quoit back and forth to each other across the net for an hour until we were warmed up and well exercised.

This was an early and primitive example of the indoor club. Others which I visited later offered devotees more space and amenities: separate dressing-rooms, showers and above all rooms fitted with a battery of ultra-violet lamps beneath which one could lie, wearing goggles, in an effort to preserve the summer's tan. This always seemed to me to provide the only sensible excuse for continuing indoors in winter a pursuit whose proper place, if it had one at all, was the open air.

Sidney Williams was a great believer in the therapeutic value of light and air on the human skin. His own, ever since he started yachting, was always beautifully pigmented and after a week-end in the sun he would proudly unbutton his shirt to display his dark brown chest. When I was with him, and when the weather permitted, I needed no encouragement to strip down to a pair of shorts; and when we swam, well out to sea miles from the crowded holiday beaches, there was naturally no need even for a decent minimum. To be towed along at seven or eight knots behind the ship, holding on to a life-belt at the end of a rope, provided the most exquisite sensation of all.

The skipper might perhaps have been persuaded, if he had not preferred the unpeopled sea, to have gone with me one day to one of the many idyllic sylvan playgrounds round London which I discovered; but the idea of indoor gatherings of naked people, where the men outnumbered the women and the middle aged men outnumbered the young ones, was altogether too kinky for him. Certainly, although he was fond of ballroom dancing, he thought that dancing in the nude, as they did at one establishment at Finchley, was going too far, even though it took place, as I assured him it did, without the slightest impropriety. The proprietor of a very well conducted club in North Kensington, centred upon the ultra-violet lamps, told me that at one house where nudists danced something not far short of an orgy developed and he himself would have none of it. At all the clubs I visited, before I lost both my inclination and my figure, the atmosphere and the proceedings were as respectable as, if very different from, those at any vicarage garden party. But most people who have passed their youth look more attractive dressed than undressed and it is the beauty of the children, for whom nakedness is always natural and right, that I chiefly remember.

So I told my stories as we lay in the sun behind the canvas wind-break, while Sidney's strong blunt fingers, never idle for long, were busy cleaning a vital part of the engine or practising knots and splices. We listened to every news bulletin from the B.B.C., which told us of the Italian invasion of Albania. And Sidney in his turn talked about New Court and the partners and our colleagues, about finance and economics, and in a fatherly way about my own career. He said once, not long after I joined his department, that sooner or later it would be discovered whether or not I read the *Financial Times* every day. This was before the paper included the outstandingly good review of the arts which are a feature of it today and I had admitted to being bored by the financial, commercial and industrial matters of which it was mainly composed. Although I modified my attitude as I grew older, more sensible and more deeply involved in my job, I was never able wholly to rid myself of the feeling that there was something slightly indecent in the spectacle of a young man poring over the financial papers. This narrow and short-sighted view did not seem to me to be inconsistent with an earnest determination to learn my job thoroughly and to perfect myself in its technique. But the fundamental folly of an exclusive concentration on trees to the neglect of the wood and of a frivolous contempt for the dreary science, was only too apparent to Sidney. He pointed out prophetically that such behaviour would, to say the least, be a hindrance if I wanted to achieve a really successful career in the City; and if that were not my objective what was I doing at New Court at all? Surely I would not be content to be another X or another Y, to get so far and never any farther?

This lesson, it is to be feared, was not fully learned. In the meantime, however, the skipper taught me other things of a more practical kind which I was to find useful—not indeed at New Court, but soon and in circumstances quite unforeseen. By that last Easter I had ceased to be merely a passenger in the ship and become a reasonably competent deck-hand who could be trusted not to bump the side too violently with the dinghy or to lay the anchor in such a way that it would drag in the night.

The time came when we had to head for home and face that still stiff and icy east wind. I was entrusted with the wheel. Having crammed on every article of clothing I had brought with me and an oilskin over all I steered the ship across Christ-church Bay, while she pitched into the waves and flung freezing spray like grape-shot into my face. It was extremely uncomfortable and at the same time exhilarating. At last we reached our mooring and stretched the canvas cover tightly over the cockpit; in a few minutes the Valor Perfection stove raised the temperature in the saloon to a snug 70°. Sidney lit the primus and cooked the last dinner aboard, while I brushed the dried salt from my face and glowed with well-being.

A week or two later, when my non-official mind was thinking back to nautical lore and forward to the question of war service, I met a man in the City who suggested a way by which the two might be combined. The authorities at New Court had agreed not to claim that I was in a reserved occupation; Brooks, only fifty-five and with unabated vigour, was ready to carry on by himself in an emergency. I assumed correctly that the R.N.V.R. was impenetrable. John Lang, a friend of my brother and a yachtsman even more serious than Sidney Williams in the sense that he was devoted to sail and despised marine motoring, told me about the River Emergency Service, which seemed the next best thing.

This body, which was being recruited by the Port of London Authority from members of yacht clubs and others who were accustomed to handling small power-boats in a tideway, was in essence an Air-Raid Precautions service for the floating population of the Thames from the estuary to Teddington and for installations on the banks of the river which could not be conveniently looked after by the riparian authorities. The P.L.A.

chartered boats from owners who were prepared not only to serve but also to captain their own craft; others like myself who were without ships but who nevertheless had some experience were welcomed as crew. Mine was limited but happily I was not called upon to undergo any practical or other test before being enrolled.

On a Sunday in July 1939 an all-day exercise took place, the only one in which I participated between the date on which I joined the service and that on which I was called up. It reminded me strongly of O.T.C. field-days when I was at school, since at no time did I have even a vague notion of the overall plan, of my part in it or of anything that was going on outside my own area of vision. I was transported from Tower Pier to Dagenham early in the morning and back again in the evening; the intervening hours I spent with two or three others equally at a loss sheltering from the chill of an English summer in the warmth of the Ford factory.

Back at New Court I found a keenly interested listener in Lionel, a yachtsman on the grand scale himself, who on hearing all about the R.E.S. promptly and generously offered his launch *Nigella*, *Rhodora II*'s tender. I was disappointed at first when the offer could not be accepted but on reflection I was relieved that I did not have to accept any even indirect responsibility for this beautiful vessel and I feel sure that Lionel, too, was thankful that he did not have to entrust her in the crowded river to an amateur crew.

On Friday, 1 September, while we were standing round the tape-machine in the front-hall reading of the invasion of Poland, a telegram arrived instructing me to report for duty the following day. On Saturday I duly repaired to Greenwich, where my ship was tied up at the pier. No uniform was provided; I was wearing the regulation gear of a dark blue reefer jacket with black anchor buttons and a white-topped yachting cap which I had bought from Gardiner's. Special R.E.S. cap badges were issued later; for the time being, disliking the appearance of my cap without a badge, I wore that of the Little Ship Club, which was very pretty but to which I regret to say I had no right. A very strange episode in my life had begun.

We were quartered in the Ship Hotel, to which in days gone by the nobility and gentry had resorted for whitebait suppers but which was now just another pub and a rather squalid one at that. My skipper, Val Langford, whose wife was also a member of the crew, invited me to sleep on board his ship, a twin-screw cruiser rather larger than *Sirius*. I bunked down in a tiny cabin which, cramped and comfortless as it was, at least saved me from a palliasse in the *ad hoc* dormitory.

On Sunday morning, 3 September, it fell to me to remain on watch while the others on the station went into the pub to listen to Chamberlain's broadcast and thereafter to make plans for organization and duty rosters. When the sirens sounded I was panic-stricken. All that I had ever read or heard of the likelihood of a single, massive, all-out attack from the air by which the enemy might seek to finish the war almost before it had begun swept into my mind like the sudden onset of a mortal disease. I was alone and solely responsible for the four-mile stretch of London River from Blackwall to Limehouse. What ought I to do? Why didn't everybody come running? Hadn't they heard the sirens or were they waiting until twelve o'clock so that they could have a drink before manning the boats? I did nothing, of course, and that turned out, as so often, to be the correct course.

After a short initial period of uncertainty and improvisation we settled down into some sort of fairly orderly routine. Steel helmets and service gas-masks were issued and messing arrangements made. If any senior officer visited us I did not see him and my impression is that we were left very much on our own to organize ourselves for action. But of action, during those early mild and sunny months, we saw none. We cruised up and down our reaches of the river, gradually getting to know every filthy soupy inch of the waters for which we were responsible and the docks and wharves past which they ran; we taught ourselves the ways of the fast-running tides; we practised trans-shipping bodies on stretchers from our boat to one of the river steamers which had been converted as a hospital ship. And in the evening those of us who were not on duty pub-crawled.

Our hospital ship was commanded by a retired naval officer, Commander Drummond, who had won a V.C. at Zeebrugge. He very rarely went ashore and when his ship was tied up alongside us to the floating pontoon at Greenwich Pier he remained on board in his cabin endlessly playing a penny whistle. Nobody got to know him very well but his plaintive warbling in the stillness of the evening watch will always be remembered.

Memorable, too, in the absence of incidents of greater import, were the pubs in Greenwich, strange out-of-the-way houses in grimy back-streets to which we found our way through the blackout, and others on the Isle of Dogs across the river to which we tramped through the echoing tunnel. In one dingy little bar-room stood an ancient gap-toothed piano like an ugly and battered pugilist who had survived a thousand bouts and was still game for a few undemanding rounds. As soon as I had struck a few notes on the stained keys men began to gather round. Until closing-time I sat there strumming every old musical-hall song I knew and making a shot at many that I didn't: 'A Bicycle Made for Two', 'My Old Dutch', 'Down at the Old Bull and Bush'—they sang lustily enough to drown my wrong notes, applauded and roared for more. Between songs I paused to lower the level in my beer mug; instantly somebody took it away and put it back refilled to add another to the countless rings on the top of the piano.

But it is above all the men we met—the dockers, the stevedores, the lightermen, the tugboatmen, men whom our normal lives in the City only a few miles away would never have brought us into contact with—it is these, and the friendly way in which they welcomed us to their river and their pubs, who made that interlude uniquely fascinating. One whom I remember in particular was the master of a wreck-lighter, a squat, thick-necked bollard of a man, not young, with something of the massive strength of the ungraceful vessel he commanded. To him, it was clear, I was a person with some education and

wisdom who nevertheless, in spite of a rather la-di-da voice, was
not lacking in human warmth; moreover I was wearing not a
forbidding white collar and well-pressed suit but a fisherman's
blue jersey and a pair of trousers as oil-stained and shapeless as
his own. Having a personal problem on his hands which he did
not know how to solve, he therefore drew me on one side and
asked for my advice. He began to explain the difficulty but had
not reached the point by closing-time and we arranged to meet
the following day on the pier. The trouble was that he had no
facility with words, which he used with almost as much awkwardness and incompetence as I should have shown if I had
ever been called upon to handle his lighter and the heavy
unfamiliar gear with which it was equipped. We met several
times over a period of several days. On each occasion I learned
a little more about him, his life, his job, his family and his home,
but I never came even distantly in sight of the problem or its
nature, whether social, legal, matrimonial or whatever. Finally
he was called away from Greenwich to another part of the river
and I never saw him again.

From time to time, feeling very much an old sea-dog, I made
the short journey to New Court to see Brooks and the others
who were holding the fort. They were pretty busy and inquired
whether in the absence of air-raids I really had anything useful
to do or whether I was in fact enjoying a yachting holiday.
There was no very convincing answer to their questions and in
January 1940 I arranged with Langford that for an experimen-
tal period I should try working at New Court during the day
and spending my evenings and nights at Greenwich. I generally
got back to the Ship rather late and the publican's daughter
cooked and served me dinner in the steamy warmth of the vast
basement kitchen. She was an excellent cook and always had a
good hot meal for me which I could enjoy so long as I kept my
eyes averted from the swarms of cockroaches with which the
angle between walls and ceiling were festooned. The arrangement for part-time service did not work very well and after a
few weeks I resigned altogether. The episode was over, and as if
to symbolize its conclusion the dirty and unlamented pub was

completely destroyed a little later by a direct hit. But it was not the end of the R.E.S., of course; indeed it was in a real sense the beginning, for after my departure the service was reorganized and by the time there was real work for it to do it had been converted from a rag-time party of happy-go-lucky amateurs into a disciplined and efficient force.

New Court in war-time was a fortress manned only by a small garrison of men whose presence in the City was necessary to keep the place going. The young men had been called up; the women and those of the older men whose jobs could be done conveniently in the country were evacuated to the mansion at Tring in Hertfordshire where the second Lord Rothschild had kept his entomological collection. In the Dividend Office coupons and drawn bonds were still taken in over the counter but were then immediately conveyed to Tring for processing. Brooks remained staunchly at the helm during the day and commanded the fire-watchers by night. During the daylight alerts we descended to the basement and sat on tin boxes in the stone-flagged passages until the sound of the 'all clear'. The efficiency of the New Court fire brigade saved the building from destruction by incendiary bombs; it could not have protected us from the high explosives which flattened wide areas of the City all round us. Throughout the war New Court suffered nothing worse than windows broken and doors blown in by blast and the superficial damage to the roof which the incendiaries inflicted in the few seconds before the watchers got to them. The building and our jobs were still there when we came back to them.

On Sundays, to relieve the regular staff, a few of us worked in rotation at the Royal Mint Refinery, where some of the plant had been turned over to the manufacture of precision parts for artillery. We were employed on the unskilled but exhausting task of putting swarf through the magnetting machines, which separated the ferrous from the non-ferrous metal among the sweepings from the factory floor.

But I was still on the look-out for a proper war-time job which would put me into regulation uniform. The next one I found was the cause of considerable mirth among my friends in the Foreign Exchange Department and to Sidney Williams in particular. Commissions were being offered in the Administrative and Special Duties branch of the Royal Air Force Volunteer Reserve. I sent in my application supported by a letter from the firm, signed by Anthony de Rothschild, in which he said that I had been a member of their staff for some fifteen years and during recent years had occupied a position of responsibility. Generously he added: 'We have a high opinion here of his ability and general integrity and we feel sure that he will carry out any duties entrusted to him efficiently and conscientiously. Although Mr Palin's position with us renders him at present exempt from military service, we are quite ready to release him should his application be granted.'

This resulted quickly in my being summoned to the Air Ministry for an interview. The selection committee, arrayed formally at a long table, were courteous and friendly but were obviously disappointed to discover that although I could claim to be a manager in a bank I was not actually a bank manager, which so far as candidates from the banking world were concerned appeared to be the only qualification which fitted one for the administrative branch. They shook their heads regretfully. And then, in response to a final question about my job, I began talking about foreign exchange. Their eyes lit up; this was more like it. Did I really know all about foreign currencies and exchange rates? Yes, sir. Well then, I ought to be an Accountant Officer. Perhaps I would like to go and see Squadron-Leader So-and-so. Fine, I said. They gave me the number of his room; I found it, knocked and went in. Two officers were sitting at either side of a plain deal table. I explained the circumstances and in three minutes, without any more formalities of any kind, the two agreed to recommend me for a commission which they assured me I could take for granted would go through. The letter of confirmation duly arrived and a few weeks later, in November 1940, I had bought my uniform and was on my way, an Acting Pilot Officer, to the Equipment and Accountant Officers' School at Grange-over-Sands in

Lancashire. That I had achieved this by representing myself to be a currency expert was for Sidney the best joke of the war.

In January 1941, towards the end of the six weeks' course, I wrote to my cousin Anthony Palin, the ophthalmic surgeon, who was also in the R.A.F. and a member of the medical staff at Halton, to ask if there was a chance of my being posted to the same station. It would be pleasant to be with him; in addition to that Halton was not only a former Rothschild estate but situated in my own home county of Buckinghamshire. If there was a vacancy there for an accountant officer, perhaps my cousin could drop a word in the appropriate ear. I had no reply and when the list of postings came through Halton was not among them. I chose Stanmore as being the only station on the list which was in the London area. Twenty-four hours after the list of names and stations had been reported to the Air Ministry a signal arrived from them changing my posting from Stanmore to Halton. As soon as I arrived there I sought out my cousin and thanked him for his timely and effective intervention. He was surprised to see me and told me that he had not received my letter and had therefore taken no action in the matter. It was difficult to believe either that Divine Providence, in spite of more pressing concerns, had taken a hand or that the occurrence was due solely to pure chance, but no other explanation was ever forthcoming.

The R.A.F. station at Halton was one of the biggest in the country; it comprised not only the School of Technical Training, in which some ten thousand apprentices were taught to be fitters and riggers, but also a School of Cookery, a hospital and a medical reception centre. Alfred de Rothschild's mansion was the officers' mess, to which a new wing containing bedrooms and bathrooms had been added. The medical profession was well, according to some people over, represented and doctors of various kinds, whether permanently stationed at Halton or just passing through, abounded. They were instantly recognizable by the gilt badges on the lapels of their uniform jackets which innocent laymen like me were told represented a spirochaete.

The headquarters staff of administrative, technical, equipment and accountant officers, who had their own private ante-room, was comparatively small. Most of the senior officers on the permanent staff lived out and were not much seen in Halton House itself except at lunch. The mess employed a paid professional mess secretary of great resource who fed us extremely well, producing such dishes as roast cygnet and pickled peaches to vary the standard rations. The sleeping quarters were comfortable, almost luxurious. There were tennis courts and a pavilion in which dances were held from time to time with the nurses and W.A.A.F. officers. All in all life at Halton was agreeable, almost shockingly so for war-time, but unhappily the work I had to do, although no doubt necessary, was monotonous and unexciting.

The Equipment Accounts Section consisted of twenty-odd airmen, W.A.A.F.s and civilian clerks who were housed in a large wooden hut in one corner of which was my own office. It was efficiently run by a Flight-Sergeant who had been doing the job for many years and naturally knew a good deal more about it than I had learned during my course. There was little for me to do but sign my name hundreds of times a day on the forms and vouchers which were put in front of me and which authorized or recorded the movement of stores and equipment of every kind into and out of the station or from one part of it to another. Of every kind, that is, except actual aircraft, for Halton was not an operational station and although it did possess an airfield very little flying took place. The absence of any action made our work seem rather remote and unreal and although it would be silly to pretend that I envied the friends in my branch of the service who were doing the same job at, for example, Biggin Hill or Manston or Tangmere I certainly felt that they were making a more serious contribution to the war effort and was rather ashamed of the tranquillity of my days and nights.

All the other accountant officers, six in number, were in the much larger Cash Section occupied with pay and allowances. In charge was a Group-Captain, one of the very few in the

R.A.F. of such exalted rank, which was the highest to which a career accountant officer could aspire. On the fortnightly pay days everyone including me was roped in to take charge of the pay parades which took place all over the camp. At these the presiding officer was always an accountant officer who had to hand to each man the sum in notes and florins sung out by the sergeant or corporal who assisted him. This was a duty which so far as I was concerned caused a certain amount of anxiety. One had to assume that one had been given the correct total of money for the wing and if when the last man's name and entitlement were called out there was not, as sometimes happened, the exact sum left in the bag for him there was nothing for it but to suppose that an earlier payee had got away with too much and make up the shortage from one's own pocket. I lost two or three pounds in this way, as a result doubtless of carelessness. Somehow it never happened that one made a profit.

I also had to take my turn at drawing the money from the bank the day before the pay parades took place. This involved a jaunt into Aylesbury by car with an N.C.O., which made a pleasant break in the routine, but the orders were that one had to be armed. Although we had been given some revolver practice I still sometimes think with horror of the probable carnage among the shoppers in the crowded High Street if any hold-up had been attempted.

It did not seem at all probable that the day would come when I should be called upon to display my expertise with foreign currencies, but in the early summer it did. The Group-Captain summoned me to his office and showed me a black leather bag containing a large quantity of French francs which he said had been brought home by an R.A.F. contingent after the fall of France. These I was to take the following day, which was Saturday, to the Bank of England and hand over against the bank's receipt; in consideration of my faithful discharge of this task I could take the rest of the week-end off. This was right up my street. I procured a travel-warrant, took the bag from the safe early the next morning and an hour or two later, having successfully completed my business at the bank, I was proudly showing off my uniform at New Court. Unhappily Sidney Williams was not there for me to cast his unkind jibe in his face.

At the country office I was a regular visitor, since Tring was only a few miles from Halton. It was a grievous shock, the first time I went there, to find that Steph was a very sick man, although he was making resolute efforts to keep going. I arranged snooker matches between the two establishments and an interesting by-product of these was that a member of my R.A.F. side fell in love with and married a girl whom he met at Tring. The marriage, however, like so many contracted during the war, did not last. Sometimes I asked one of the Dividend Office girls to a Saturday night dance at the Halton tennis club and sometimes I was invited to dine at Tring, perhaps in order to demonstrate that the notion current at New Court that the evacuees were living on the fat of the land and unaffected by rationing was somewhat exaggerated. And on one occasion I went at the invitation of A. E. Kimpton to a dance given in the town hall for the staff of R.M.R. Engineering, an offshoot of the Refinery whose works were at Tring. This I took as a high honour, for I went as one of the official party which included Mr and Mrs Lionel and Lord and Lady Rothschild and no other member of the NMR staff was invited. That evening was remarkable for the contrast between the extreme decorum of the proceedings while the family was present and the riotous abandon which followed their departure.

Through the warm summer days I sat in my little room with the windows open at my back to the sound of mowing and the smell of the cut grass. There were days when there was nothing to relieve the boredom of forms and vouchers and returns; days saddened by the tears of a young W.A.A.F. whom the flight-sergeant had to bring to me apologetically in some sort of trouble; days brightened by negotiations with the railway company about demurrage which I was asked by the Group-Captain to conduct; days enlivened by visits from officers from other parts of the camp who, saluting me correctly at my door, came in for some special piece of equipment or just for a chat;

days filled only with slowly passing hours. But every day five o'clock came at last, when we thankfully closed our offices and walked together up to the mess for tea and made plans for the long evening. Then there would be tennis, followed by a leisurely hot bath and dinner; after dinner perhaps a visit to Tring or beer and darts at the Bell at Aston Clinton or billiards on one of the tables which Lionel had presented. One night a few of us drove to High Wycombe for a dance at the headquarters of Bomber Command; another night there was a concert at which Nancy Evans wrung our hearts by her singing of Schubert's 'Ungeduld'. Some nights we sat lazily on the terrace at the back of the house looking down across Alfred's garden to his huge ornamental fountain and the beech-woods beyond, midsummer nights when you could still see to read out-of-doors at eleven o'clock. And so we went to bed, with quiet minds except for the unfortunate duty officer who when his turn came round crept apprehensively to the special room set apart for him and prayed that the telephone would not ring during the night.

It is above everything else a song which brings them back, the days of that strange interlude, with their boredom, their hours of quiet happiness and companionship and their rare moments of excitement. Rummaging among the stationery in my cupboard I came across some loose sheets from a book of songs, part of the score of a musical entertainment which appeared to have been written for and sung by the apprentices in a more leisurely age. The words have mostly been forgotten and the tune is only dimly remembered, but still snatches of that sentimental little ballad run in my head, and the notes flutter down nostalgically like autumn leaves, and the gentle melancholy sweetness of it almost brings tears to my eyes when I sing it to myself with plenty of *rubato*: still it instantly recalls the long summer days at Halton and the young men for whom the war was only a little distant in space and not distant at all in time as it had been for those who had gone before them and learned about aeroplanes and sung their songs amid the woods and hills of Buckinghamshire:

When beech leaves are falling, are falling, are falling,
Wherever I'm stationed, where'er I may roam,
Old memories come calling, come calling, come calling,
Of youth's golden scenery, of Halton and home.

Chapter 11 **Berfin, Jamfin and Trifin**

In July 1941, when I had been at Halton for six months, a signal from the Air Ministry arrived on the desk of Air Commodore G. B. Dacre, the Station Commander, requesting him to arrange for Pilot Officer R. V. Palin to present himself at the War Office to see a certain naval officer. Who he? the A.O.C. may well have asked in the manner of Harold Ross. And what for? And why this strange conjunction of the three services? I had met the A.O.C., of course, but not often. The paths of the most senior and the most junior officer on the station lay far apart and since the former did not much care for the company of the medical men with whom the Officers' Mess was always infested he rarely appeared there. However, if that was what the powers at the Ministry wanted, let them have it; the matter was clearly in any case not of the slightest importance. The adjutant was ordered to contact the Senior Accountant Officer and lay it on.

The signal did not come as a surprise to me but rather as a joyous confirmation that an eventuality to which I had been eagerly looking forward for many long and tedious weeks might actually be coming to pass. I had been at Halton barely a month, the glamour of the uniform was wearing off and the tedium of my unexciting work beginning to eat into my soul, when Hilary Scott telephoned. He spoke cagily but the general tenor of his remarks was clear: he had mentioned my name to Geoffrey Vickers, had been encouraged by him, and had discovered my present whereabouts from Brooks: now he was able to hint darkly but unmistakably that unless I was indissolubly wedded to the R.A.F. I might like to consider a job of a quite different kind, one in which there might be scope for the application of the specialized knowledge which I had acquired at New Court.

The invitation, hedged about though it might be with 'ifs' and 'buts', could not have been more timely. I responded enthusiastically. But Vickers had almost immediately to go abroad and it was not until May 1941 that he was able to write to me himself and explain what it was all about. He had been appointed a director of the Ministry of Economic Warfare where there was 'a job for which someone of your qualifications is badly needed. Unless,' he went on, 'you have now found a really good niche I think there is a post here where you could be very usefully occupied in winning the war. Is there any chance of seeing you?'

His letter, after the long silence and the gradual fading of hope, came like an order of release. Before I could see Vickers himself he had to leave the country again, but he set everything in train before his departure; the signal came from the Air Ministry and I duly reported to the War Office. On my way to the room in which the interview was to take place I passed the open door of another office in which Hugh Quennell was installed; I had always thought that Slaughter and May were a wonderful firm in peace-time and now it seemed they were running the war. The meeting at the War Office was followed by one with Dudley Ward at M.E.W. in Berkeley Square House and shortly after my return to Halton I received letters informally from him and formally from the Establishment Department offering me a post at the British Embassy in Washington. I should have diplomatic status, with the rank of Second Secretary, and I must resign my commission immediately with a view to leaving for the United States at the earliest possible moment after a brief period of indoctrination at the Ministry.

Group-Captain Wiseman was not very pleased when he heard my news. Torn between his reluctance to lose even a junior and not specially competent member of his staff and his feeling that it would be absurd to stress the importance of my contribution to the work of the Accounts Section, he confined himself to warning me of the high cost of living in Washington. He named a figure of £5 per day as what in his opinion I should need to maintain myself there, but happily I was able to reassure him that that was almost exactly what I was to receive by way of pay and allowances.

We then turned to the procedure for resigning my commission. He advised me about the correct language to use in my letter and the channels through which it must pass. I must write formally to the A.O.C. and request him to submit my application, which would go according to the rules from him to Group, from Group to Technical Training Command and from Command to the Air Ministry. I wrote; I waited; nothing happened. Hearing nothing M.E.W. inquired the reason. My letter had got stuck in somebody's 'in' tray. I did not doubt that my friends Flight Lieutenants Thorp and Catchpole, respectively the Station Adjutant and Assistant Station Adjutant at Halton, had played their part expeditiously but it was hardly to be expected that their opposite numbers at Group and at Command would be equally conscious of the importance at this juncture of rapid action. So M.E.W. started prodding from the other end of the line. They asked Air Ministry, who asked Command, who asked Group: where was this man Palin's letter of resignation? Ultimately they sorted it out between them; the letter was traced and the resignation accepted. I was out.

The order of release came only just in time to save me from what would certainly have proved to be a hideous chore. The annual audit of the 'non-public' accounts—those, that is to say, of the officers', warrant officers' and sergeants' messes, of the station cinema and of various clubs and similar organizations not financed from public funds—was due to be carried out and station orders that week gave the names of the accountant officers to whom they were allocated. The sight of my name against two of them gave me the sort of feeling with which one might hear of the derailment in a tunnel of a tube-train from which one had alighted at the previous station.

My last act at Halton after a round of good-byes was to sell my uniforms to two officers of about my size who were in need of spares. Wearing my best blue for the last time I drove over light-heartedly to Tring to bid farewell to the boys and girls of NMR who were carrying on bravely in the mansion. Thankful afterwards that I had done so I sought out Lionel de Rothschild, who was in residence, little thinking that I should never see him again.

When news of the, to me, utterly unexpected death of the senior partner reached me in Washington six months later every detail of that cosy interview in his sitting-room at Tring came back. It was a little oasis of peace and stillness, like the head-master's study at a co-educational boarding-school into which the sound of the distant shouting and laughter of the pupils at play in the evening faintly penetrated. Lionel was sitting in an armchair drawn up close to the fire, although it was a warm summer night. He put down his book and for half an hour we chatted about New Court and my career and the new life and work that awaited me. He looked forward to my return to NMR when the war was over. He was genial, friendly, interested in me personally, a very different Lionel from the aloof and formidable figure of earlier days. But he was also unusually quiet and sub-dued. It did not occur to me until later that he was already ill. He died in January 1942, a few days after his sixtieth birthday.

On Monday, 11 August 1941, I reported to M.E.W. in Berkeley Square and sat for a week at the feet of Harry Lucas in the section of the Ministry called 'Financial Pressure', talking to him when he had time, reading his telegrams, trying to form some sort of picture of his esoteric activities, meeting the delight-fully named Ernest Bliss and others with whom I should be in correspondence and eating strange meals in the canteen. On Monday, 18 August, I took train to Liverpool and slept at the Adelphi Hotel. The following morning I embarked in a small Norwegian freighter of 3,000 tons for Canada. On Monday, 25 August, six days after leaving the Mersey, we entered the Strait of Belle Isle between Newfoundland and Labrador and sighted land.

It was a voyage remarkable only for the fact that after the first day out, when an Anson reconnaissance plane flew low over us and a large convoy appeared in the distance, we saw nothing but sea and sky. Remembering my first Atlantic crossing in the *Aquitania* I was taken aback by the diminutive size of the ship when I first saw her at the quay. Unconvoyed, not zigzagging, blacked out during the short nights, we went straight across, hell for leather. After we had reached the open sea I spent the next forty-eight hours lying prone on my bunk eating oranges and dry biscuits. Then I rose refreshed and joined the other passengers, thereafter not missing a single plentiful course. There were eleven of us: one other civilian with whom I shared a cabin; four young R.A.F. pilots who were going to Canada as flying instructors; four Merchant Navy officers on their way to join another ship, having had their previous one torpedoed under them in the south Atlantic; and finally a Canadian officer in the British Army going home on leave. We all sat at one table in the dining saloon where we were joined by the Norwegian captain, who had also been torpedoed at the outset of the German invasion of Norway. None of the other ship's officers appeared. The ship being refrigerated and provisioned in Canada we were well supplied with fresh fruit, butter and cheese; tinned milk was the only item to grumble about. Apart from a primitive shuffle-board there was nothing whatever to amuse ourselves with and we spent our time sitting in the small smoking-room drinking and yarning. Those who liked Scotch whisky were pleased to find that they could get it for only ten shillings a bottle; I concentrated on beer which came up ice-cold in tins looking as though they contained metal-polish but which tasted like Pilsner. In the telling of tales the other civilian and I did our best to compete with the more stirring experiences of the seamen and airmen who had seen real action.

The Canadian coast came into view bringing an Arctic chill in the wind and the beautiful menace of massive icebergs which had floated down from the north and stranded in the shallows. Then we lost sight of land again for a day as we crossed the vast gulf of St Lawrence. At Farther Point, where the great river narrowed to about forty miles, the pilot came aboard. A broken exhaust valve delayed us for some hours at anchor and we did not reach Quebec until after dark.

It was the first time for two years that any of us had seen a city illuminated at night. We lined the rail gazing entranced at the floodlit Montmorency Falls, the Heights of Abraham and the imposing pile of the Château Frontenac. As we approached Quebec Bridge it seemed that the ship's masts must be snapped off like carrots but we passed safely underneath with forty feet to spare. We turned in for the last night on board, certain at last that we should sleep undisturbed. The ship rumbled evenly up the river and when we awoke we were in Montreal.

The unfinished city, that strange Franco-British-American hotch-potch, became so familiar to me in later years when I was there continually on the business of NMR that first impressions are difficult to distinguish from the subsequent ones by which they were thickly overlaid. In addition my mind, now that I was on the North American continent, was beginning more and more to be filled with thoughts of the job which I had been brought so far and at such expense to do. It was certainly a British city at war that young Deakin, my cabin-mate, and I briefly explored. Union Jacks and V-signs were to be seen on every hand and the shop windows were full of pictures of the King and Winston Churchill. Deakin, it now emerged, was to travel south by the same train as I, leaving Montreal at 9 p.m., but to leave it at New York. He even went so far as to admit, now that enemy submarines were no longer listening, that he was to take up a post not unconnected with the Ministry of Information. We dropped our bags at the station, had them cleared through U.S. customs and then decided upon a hair-cut and shampoo, for which we were appalled to have to pay the equivalent of seven and sixpence. We sent off cables to those who we considered might be interested to hear of our safe arrival, roamed around some more and finally met our R.A.F. and Merchant Navy friends in the comfortable oak-panelled bar of the Queen's Hotel. The fliers had been to H.Q. to discover their several remote and outlandish destinations and after lunch we put them in their trains for Moose Jaw or Medicine Hat. After more rubber-necking, more drinks and another meal Deakin and I entered our sleeper to experience for the first time the contortions of a mode of travel previously known only from the movies.

After a night punctuated by frequent stops and violent jerks as the coupling system took up the slack we awoke to find the sun shining on the woods and fields and white frame-houses of Connecticut. As we finished breakfast we rolled into New York City through the back-door, denied the unique spectacle of the skyscrapers given to those arriving by sea. Deakin left me and I settled down alone for the last four-hour lap through Philadelphia, Wilmington and Baltimore, past broad rivers and groves of wild sumach and ugly little towns, to the capital.

Without any conscious intention of doing so I immediately created a record by walking the entire distance from Union Station to His Britannic Majesty's Embassy, something which, as I learned afterwards, had never been done before. There was no one to meet me; it was two o'clock in the afternoon and it seemed likely that if I turned up in a few minutes by taxi I should find everybody at lunch. So I deposited my luggage in the cloak-room, consulted a street plan of the city, found the beginnings of Massachusetts Avenue, and undaunted by the fact that the Embassy's address was No. 3100, set out on foot. The distance, as I should have realized, was over three miles; the temperature was 89° and still rising. My suit was of a weight suitable for an English summer.

I had been warned that economic warriors were housed not in the Chancery but in a temporary building which had been put up in the grounds for what was known as the War Trade Department. I did not, therefore, make the mistake of presenting myself at Lutyens's embassy itself, which looked as if it had been lifted out of the Hampstead Garden Suburb and had swollen considerably in the process, but went round to the War Tradesmen's entrance. Here I was received with characteristic warmth by Bobbie Stopford, a Counsellor and my immediate chief, who was no stranger since I had met him in the City when he ran various Hungarian creditors' committees; with similar expressions of joy by Bill Ritchie, who was another Second Secretary, another old friend and another lawyer from the ubiquitous firm of Slaughter and May; and with profuse apologies by young Quentin Keynes, a nephew of the great economist, who was the section's general assistant and factotum. Quentin had been sent in his huge, thirsty motor-car to meet me at the station but had somehow contrived to miss me. The section was completed, so far as concerned those on the diplomatic list, by Jack Auburn, a New Zealander, who had arranged for me to use his house in Cleveland Avenue while he was away on holiday, and by Quintin Bridge, the tallest man in the Embassy, who arrived from England shortly after me and became one of my closest friends. Jack was a professional banker of long experience, having spent most of his working life with the Manufacturers Trust Company. Quintin was also a banker, from Seligman Brothers, but more of an amateur; he had devoted his lively and adaptable mind to a number of different activities in his time, including photography, in which he displayed brilliant artistry. The group was supported by secretaries and clerical assistants of both sexes, many of them Canadians.

After a night in the Wardman Park Hotel and reunion with my luggage I moved into Jack Auburn's house and began quickly to look round for one of my own. I found it in Woodley Road. Although it was the property of an architect, who was moving to Ohio and agreed to let it to me furnished for the sum of $1,500 a year, it was an ugly red-brick Victorian-type villa, joined to its similar neighbours on both sides and furnished and decorated with a complete absence of taste of any kind, even bad. However, it provided the necessities for modest comfort, was centrally heated, though not air-conditioned, and lay within ten minutes' walk of the Embassy in the leafy northwest part of the city.

While I was completing the formalities I heard of the impending arrival of a young man called H. W. R. Wade, who was coming from the Treasury to work with the Financial Attaché.

I met him at the airport and invited him to share the house with me. Although no more impressed with it from an aesthetic point of view than I was, he had nowhere else to go and had no hesitation in agreeing to what seemed to be an admirable arrangement. He noted with approval that the house had a garage opening on to the alley at the back. Having spent some years at Harvard Law School he was sufficiently Americanized to find life insupportable without a vehicle and his first act after we moved in was to take me to a used car lot where we chose and he bought an enormous open Packard coupé or two-seater with a dickey-seat which I learned to call the rumble. Our next act was to acquire the services of a leggy young Negress called Mary Edmunds who for the sum of $10 a week plus car-fare of $1·25 came in every morning except Sunday at eight o'clock, prepared our breakfast, lunch and dinner and kept the house clean and tidy.

Bill Wade, a few years younger than I, although concerned in Washington with mainly financial matters, was a lawyer by trade and is in fact at the time of writing Professor of Law at Oxford University. Again I found myself in the closest contact with a legal mind, but this time it was that of an academic lawyer and my life-long experience of the fraternity was thus further enlarged. We got on extremely well and a solid basis of affection and shared interests was established. Among many common tastes was a love of, indeed a positive need for, music and although the piano we found in the house was a disappointment, having been allowed to deteriorate so much as to be barely playable, we soothed our savage breasts in the evening with a third acquisition in the form of a radio-gramophone. Finally we bought a few coloured prints in order to lend a little decorative brightness to our drab rooms. At last we had something we could call a home and were able to settle down undistractedly to our respective jobs.

My room was on the first floor of the War Trade annex (or the second floor when Americans visited me). It was small but not too small. It contained a desk and two or three chairs, a separate table for putting things on, a secure steel cupboard, a waste-paper basket, another receptacle for secret waste and, most important of all, an air-conditioner. This was a box the size of a small suitcase which fitted into the permanently closed window, hummed unobtrusively and kept the room at a comfortable 70° while the summer temperature outside was twenty or thirty degrees higher. My secretary was a capable and attractive Canadian girl called Sheila Bowen who changed her name to Sheila Fisk a year later but whose husband in the Canadian army I never met.

Walking round the annex and the Chancery to introduce myself I was much astonished to find how many people whom I had never seen before appeared to know of me. 'Ah, yes,' they said pleasantly, 'we've heard a lot about you.' At first I supposed that word had got around of my unprecedented feat in arriving on foot from the station in the tropical heat and humidity of a Washington August. But this was not at all what they meant and in fact such behaviour could earn one a reputation only for eccentricity bordering upon madness. No, it really seemed, to my amazement, that my name had been mentioned by some person or persons unknown as that of a man who might be expected to make a significant contribution on the economic front. I remembered the flattering words of Geoffrey Vickers when he first wrote to me. He had been in Washington; could it be that he, thinking of the midnight oil which we had burned together in the Old Room and of our wrestling together with Latin American Financial problems, had found time on a busy tour to speak of something so unimportant? It did not seem likely; but if not he, who? The mystery was never solved and since I did not see Vickers on a single occasion throughout my three years and four months at the Embassy I did not have an opportunity of interrogating him. When I did set eyes on him again it was 1946, I was back at New Court, he had left Slaughter and May for the National Coal Board and the whole matter had lost what little interest it once had.

Another surprising discovery was that even in a mission which as well as the noble Ambassador included six Ministers and seven or eight Counsellors, to say nothing of numerous First

Secretaries, even Second and Third Secretaries were people of some importance. They carried the same diplomatic passes signed by the Secretary of State; their cars bore diplomatic number-plates; they could initial telegrams which the Cypher Room could transmit without question. Coming from New Court, where in spite of Anthony's generous letter to the Air Ministry I had still been only a boy who might just possibly amount to something one day, I found this rather gratifying. And it was agreeable, too, to be more or less one's own master: one did not have to keep to fixed hours of work, to account for one's every movement or to refer to higher authority before taking any action. Although each of us worked to a considerable extent on his own, all letters, telegrams and minutes were circulated; the daily folder kept everybody informed about what everybody else was up to and also enabled Bobbie Stopford both to keep a check on us and to measure our productivity. For anyone who came as new to the game as I did a check was certainly necessary but to avoid getting on to too high a plane we adopted the useful practice of writing mainly so-called 'demi-official' letters. I knew, or soon got to know, my contacts in the various South American Embassies or legations and was glad to use the uninhibiting form of 'dear Walter' or 'dear John' correspondence. This was something which used to be frowned on in the City and appeared to be new to Americans, who were also unacquainted, it appeared, with the convenient 'dear Department' or 'dear Chancery' letter long familiar in the British Foreign Service. When a chap in the State Department wrote to a chap in one of their foreign missions he customarily addressed himself formally to the ambassador and started off: 'Sir, I am instructed by the Secretary of State . . .'. From my point of view the advantage of an informal 'dear Ted' letter was not simply that I could dispense with stiff diplomatic language but that the recipient was likewise absolved from the necessity of pulling any punches in his reply. Ted could say, for example: 'Dear Ronnie, I have investigated the man whom you suspect of being a high-powered enemy agent and he turns out to be an illiterate half-breed; the office which looks to you like the centre of Axis financial operations in the sub-continent is in fact just a hole in the wall.'

We were kept extremely busy and on six days out of the seven we started at nine o'clock and rarely left before seven. For the benefit of those who may wonder what we were doing all this time and would like to know in simple language and without too much boring detail what 'financial pressure' was and how it was exercised, it may be said briefly of my own efforts that they were directed towards denying the enemy financial succour in Latin America and severing his financial pipe-lines with that part of the world. This we sought to achieve, in conjunction with U.S. government agencies, by persuading Latin American countries to institute and enforce Trading with the Enemy legislation similar to our own and by freezing the funds of and blacklisting companies and persons in those countries who had financial dealings with the enemy.

One of our main sources of information was the censorship; not the kind of censorship which was concerned with obscenity and used to be exercised in the theatrical world by the Lord Chamberlain, but the kind which command of the seas and the 'navicert' system enabled the United Kingdom to exercise over postal and telegraphic communications. Reading other people's mail and when necessary suppressing it was an ungentlemanly and distasteful business but not more so, it may be argued, than many other activities which all-out war involved. Since it was an exclusively war-time affair no such thing as a corps of trained professional censors existed and it was remarkable that men who had demonstrated ability in quite different walks of life were found to run this complex and widespread organization.

The Director-General of the Postal and Telegraph Censorship Department throughout the war was Sir Edwin Herbert, who became Lord Tangley. He was a City solicitor and an expert on investment trusts; I had run into him once or twice when I was juggling with a security in which one of his trusts was interested. One had not suspected him then, from his mild, quiet and courteous manner, of possessing a positive genius for administration which enabled him to run his vast empire with such consummate efficiency.

In the western hemisphere the boss was Charles des Graz, who came even more improbably to the world of censorship, as he had done in the first war, from that of old books, on which he was Sotheby's chief expert. He was a tall man with a large pale face and the appearance of having only one long, fang-like tooth; this gave him a somewhat sinister look which would have enabled him to impersonate Dracula more convincingly than I had done on board the *Almeda Star*. In fact he must have been more fully equipped, since few people I ever met ate a good dinner with greater gusto. Between 1914 and 1918 Charles had been censor of American mails at the War Office. At this time Stephany as a young man had been in the correspondence department at New Court under Nauheim and had been much puzzled and annoyed by the persistent failure of one of our New York banking correspondents to act upon cabled payment orders which he sent them. After diligent inquiries it was discovered that his cables had been suppressed by a junior censor who was convinced that an institution called the Central Hanover Bank must be German. Unfortunately I did not hear about this *bêtise* until it was too late for me to scold Charles.

The banking world contributed to the censorship Anthony Acton, who came from Lazards and was financial adviser in London, and Willie Hill-Wood, a partner in Morgan Grenfell and financial adviser in the western area. Charles and Willie had decided at the outset that Washington was a place which they were quite prepared to visit as often as was necessary but not to live in. They accordingly established their office in New York, where much more was going on than just the business of government and diplomacy, as in the capital, and where they could lead fuller lives. This was an arrangement for which I personally was grateful, for I had to confer with the pair of them regularly and was thus provided with the perfect excuse for frequent visits to New York. They got on extremely well with each other and I with both. They were inseparable, at any rate until the evening when their active social lives began, and when they came down to Washington it was always together: Charles tall and dark, with his lively humour well concealed behind his rather forbidding exterior; Willie small and ruddy and cheerful, with curly ginger hair and the figure of a quondam athlete proper to a member of a famous family of cricketers. Their oddly contrasted figures became familiar in the corridors of the Embassy not only to me but to many others who if they had had any idea what the two of them were up to would doubtless have strongly disapproved.

The head of the United States Office of Censorship was a newspaperman from Indiana called Byron Price. He had a peculiarity which I remember with admiration and envy: he so arranged his official life that he never had anything on his desk. He occupied a large room in a building in downtown Washington, in which he sat with his back to the windows before a large table upon whose glass-covered top, about twenty-five square feet in area, nothing ever lay: no papers, no trays, no inkstand, no blotter; nothing. Documents requiring to be read or signed by him were brought to him and if he could not deal with them at once they were taken away; they were never left before him. It struck me as a pleasant uncluttered way to live. Several times I tried to emulate it at New Court but never with more than partial or temporary success.

With Byron Price himself I had little direct contact but one meeting which I attended with him in his office was something of a high-spot. Word reached me one day that Dingle Foot, M.P., who was then Parliamentary Secretary to M.E.W., was coming to Washington for a few days. I notified Charles des Graz, who at once set about organizing a meeting with Price for which he and Willie would come down from New York, while to me was allotted the task of bringing Foot. The point was that the Americans, although they had certainly set up an Office of Censorship and co-operated with us unreservedly, had a very creditable dislike for the whole business and were inclined to doubt whether it really made a significant contribution to the winning of the war. The opportunity was too good to miss of having a junior minister direct from London demonstrate, with examples, how mistaken this attitude was. Foot entered into the spirit of the exercise with zest. He may not have been able to dispel the Americans' natural repugnance but he certainly impressed them with his account of the vital naval and military, not just commercial and financial, information which the allies derived from intercepts.

The ugly but convenient word 'intercepts' was used for the information which reached us from the censorship stations. The foolscap sheets quoting or summarizing intercepted correspondence arrived in such vast numbers and occupied so much of the time of so many readers and sorters and registrars that even though only a small proportion of them deemed to be of special financial interest landed on my desk, and only a fraction of those called for some action on my part, they seem in retrospect to have dominated my life. Their phantasmagoric profusion, the infinite variety of subjects and persons and places they mentioned, the complicated transactions they alluded to, the patient detective work and intensive ratiocination which were required to elucidate and understand them, a process comparable to that of completing a jigsaw puzzle picture with half the pieces missing, the problem of what one could do or persuade the United States Government to do if there was good enough evidence of a financial operation which was aiding the Axis countries—all these built up over the months, when everything was new and strange, into something so much like the Lord Chancellor's nightmare song in *Iolanthe* that I was moved to compose a pastiche of Gilbert's verses. Since the scansion was unSeaman-like and the rhyming not perfectly felicitous a short extract, with explanatory notes, will be more than enough. In my M.E.W. nightmare

> I am spending my life in pursuit of a Trifin
> From a highly indelicate source,
> Which is written in gin by a left-handed Finn
> On paper unusually coarse . . . .

A Trifin (pronounced Try-fin, of course) was a financial

intercept from Trinidad, just as a Berfin was a financial intercept from Bermuda and a Jamfin one from Jamaica. When passing information so derived to the United States Treasury or the State Department one had to use a special euphemistic form of words in order not to offend their susceptibilities or cause unnecessary trouble with neutrals. One did not say: 'We gather from an intercepted letter that ...' one said always: 'We understand from a delicate source that ...'. Everybody knew perfectly well what we meant but the proprieties were thus observed.

> ... Re a man from Jamaica who's trying to take a
> Small package of French pharmaceuticals,
> Helped by beautiful spies with black hair and green eyes
> And a message in code on their cuticles.

Medicinal drugs were continually cropping up and naturally found a place in the dream. The cuticles were only dragged in for the sake of the rhyme but Willie Hill-Wood said that an incident in which an attempt was made to transmit a message written invisibly on the epidermis had actually occurred.

> The mystery grew denser when an ardent chief censor
> Examined those sinister vamps
> And discovered a pillow from Cuidad Trujillo
> Stuffed with dollars and diamonds and stamps. ...

It may be necessary today to explain that when I was young the word 'vamp' denoted an unscrupulous adventuress. Cuidad Trujillo is still the capital of the Dominican Republic. Valuable stamps occupying very little space were much used as an alternative to sending banknotes by post.

> ... Which an interested party had brought via Lati
> From sundry Castilian castles
> Where French refugees manufactured Swiss cheese
> To be sent to New York in food parcels.

Lati was an Italian air-line. It may be seen today in Alitalia flying in the opposite direction. The reference to castles in Spain was no doubt intended to convey the unreality of the operation. I don't know why food parcels should be sent to New York; presumably the idea was to sell them there for dollars, not for local consumption but to people who wanted to send a gift to friends or relations in Britain.

> Things really looked black as a man in Caracas
> Sent a cable to Vichy *en clair*,
> Which for good measure he passed to the Treasury
> As well as to Berkeley Square. . . .

Berkeley Square, it will be remembered, was the address of M.E.W. To make a dactyl of Berkeley was not so much poetic licence as poetic licentiousness.

> . . . That his wife, Ermintrude, owes ten million escudos
> To a firm of exporters in Paris
> And asked for exemption from a scheme of pre-emption
> Attributed wrongly to Marris.

The sequences of tenses is wrong here; it should, of course, be 'owed'. Currency experts will know that escudos were, and indeed still are, the currency of Portugal. Denny Marris was a Counsellor and concerned with commodities rather than finance. He was a great pre-emptor. He came to M.E.W. from Lazards, of which he is now a managing director.

> Their hearts were like flint as they shipped all his linters
> And told him politely he'd had 'em:
> For he'd foolishly sent in a form to John Dent
> Which should have been marked to Reid-Adam.

Linters cropped up frequently but I never discovered exactly what they were; some form of cotton, I believe. John Dent was another economic warrior in the field of commodities. He came from Balfour Williamson & Co., of which he became a managing director. Randle Reid-Adam was a young Commercial Secretary, the only foreign service officer in the grisly picture, who later became British Minister to the Republic of Panama.

But life in Washington in the fall of 1941 was not composed exclusively of hard work. The worst of the sticky heat gradually passed and October brought a succession of clear sunny days when no rain fell, a cool breeze rustled the trees along the broad avenues and the sumachs and maples splashed their pinks and cherry reds among the brown and gold. On Sundays we drove the Packard into the neighbouring states of Maryland and Virginia, to the Blue Ridge Mountains and the Shenandoah Valley. In the evenings the Philadelphia Symphony Orchestra played in Constitution Hall under Eugene Ormandy and on two memorable occasions under Sir Thomas Beecham and Toscanini. Rachmaninov gave one of his last public concerts and we looked forward to Kreisler, Heifetz and Rubinstein. Lauritz Melchior, Lotte Lehmann and Gracie Fields sang for us. We began to feel a little ashamed of ourselves. Were we working hard enough, and was life, even in Foggy Bottom, sometimes a little too comfortable?

And then in the afternoon of Sunday, 7 December 1941, I went for a walk round the zoo and about five o'clock entered a drug-store for a cup of coffee. The radio was loudly on and being listened to intently. For a minute I thought a highly melodramatic play was being broadcast. In fact we were hearing the first accounts of the Japanese attack on Pearl Harbor. I rushed home to Woodley Road to telephone to any of my friends who might have missed the news. America was in the war; the work increased and the tempo of our lives accelerated. Men in the embassy who had appeared to be ordinary civilians suddenly blossomed forth in the gaudy uniforms of high-ranking naval officers, soldiers and airmen. And as if to answer the charge that our lives were inappropriately luxurious Howard Johnson soon reduced from twenty-four to twelve the varieties of ice-cream which he served in his roadside restaurants and a sugar ration of $\frac{3}{4}$lb. per head per week was imposed.

Early in 1942 I enjoyed what I like to think of as my first meeting with Winston Churchill. To think of but not to write of: in a record aiming at truth it must be admitted that what took place was hardly a meeting. On the first Saturday in the new year we were invited into the Embassy ball-room after dinner to see the great man and hear a few words from him. He came in with Lord Halifax, looking pink and chubby and cheerful. Like its two or three successors it was a fairly small and intimate gathering, not an occasion for a set speech or any rhetorical fireworks. He stood in front of the fire, cigar in hand, and beamed at us for a few moments while we clapped. Then he spoke quietly and briefly, recalling the dark days of the war when we stood alone and contrasting them with the situation as it had been so recently transformed. To encourage men who were working in a theatre so far from danger and privation he stressed that everybody had a job to do and that every job was important. His eyes were half closed and almost invisible but every now and then he would open them wide, when the effect upon those standing directly in his line of vision at a distance of a few feet was of uncomfortable exposure to a penetrating pale blue searchlight.

The following day the Ambassador was asked if an opportunity could not be given to a wider circle of seeing the Prime Minister; would he not show himself for a minute or two to Embassy wives and allow them to bring their children? This Churchill sternly declined; 'What,' he is reported to have said, 'do they think I am—some kind of performing animal?'

My position in the Embassy and the nature of my work were not such as to necessitate direct contact or conference with the President and the only occasion on which I saw him at close quarters also occurred in the same month of January 1942, when he celebrated his sixtieth birthday. It was the month in which my thoughts were dragged suddenly and violently back to New Court by the announcement in the *New York Times* of the death of Lionel de Rothschild, an event which shocked me more than I should have thought possible. I sent a telegram to his brother Anthony; behind my conventional words of sympathy lay unexpressed thoughts of the surviving partner left to carry on alone and of the whole future of NMR and the part I might play in it.

Roosevelt's birthday celebrations included a performance at the National Theatre of Lilian Hellman's play *The Watch on the Rhine* in aid of his pet cause, the prevention and cure of polio. From the seat which I had been able to procure in the Embassy box just behind Lord and Lady Halifax I could see F.D.R. opposite us. He seemed in good form and high spirits. I was looking at a man who to the British was a shining hero and it was always a surprise to find how many of his own countrymen still disliked and distrusted him.

Litvinov, the Soviet Ambassador, was also in the audience. Him and his English wife I had already met when they honoured me by inviting me, along with everyone else on the diplomatic list, to a party at the Soviet Embassy on the anniversary of the October revolution. It struck me as odd that the Russians alone continued throughout the war to give diplomatic receptions on the grand scale, a form of entertainment which all the other missions had given up for the duration. As an exercise in prestige these gatherings were certainly impressive and provided temporary diplomats such as myself with some of our most glittering memories. We advanced in a dignified procession up the wide marble staircase beneath an enormous painting depicting a bloody scene at the barricades in Moscow in 1917, to be greeted at the top by His Excellency and Madame and by the sight of long tables groaning—the *cliché* cannot be avoided—under the weight of the caviar and vodka which had been flown over from the Soviet Union in gargantuan quantities for the occasion.

Lest it should be thought that I accepted this lavish hospitality without any attempt at reciprocation I must record that I did at least once succeed in getting Russian guests to a small cocktail party at my house. They were a young press attaché and his wife, named Pavlov, and although our conversation did not get beyond the stage of small-talk a cordial relationship seemed to have been established. Unfortunately the occasion was slightly marred by a flaw in my arrangements: Madame Pavlova would touch nothing but tomato juice, which by a careless oversight was the one drink I had omitted to lay in.

As a further instance, if one is needed, of the comfortable privileges which we enjoyed, I may say that we were able to import whisky from Scotland and gin from England free of duty. Even allowing for the fact that one or two bottles from each case were usually pilfered, cocktail parties could be given frequently and almost painlessly when the two staples cost only about five shillings a bottle. It was noticeable, incidentally, that although Americans were loyal and fervent in their praise of bourbon, most of them chose Scotch if it was offered to them.

Nevertheless life at New Court seemed in retrospect a picnic in comparison. Late nights in the Old Room earned us the title of 'The Midnight Follies' which was conferred on us by irreverent and ignorant persons in the General Office, but I rarely arrived much before 10.30 in the morning and could almost always count on two free days at the week-end. In the War Trade Department a sixty-hour week was normal. Visits downtown to the Treasury or the State Department became so frequent that it was no longer practicable to rely either on Bill Wade's Packard or on the car and driver placed at our disposal by the American W.V.S.: I bought for $500 a 1939 Chevrolet which when diplomatic number-plates were affixed to it seemed to me a very handsome and distinguished vehicle. I gradually ceased going home for lunch and ate in the canteen which was established in the annex and run by Embassy wives and other volunteers. Every evening when we were not entertaining or being entertained we relied on music to undo the effects of remorseless financial pressure and delight souls sickened by the spectacle of our enemies writhing in our pitiless economic grip: music from our gramophone, plaintive wood-notes from Bill's recorder and tinkling tunes from the tired but still serviceable piano on which I had expended the sum of $50.

The hard year of 1942 wore on. I went to New York to visit the Consulate-General or to confer with Charles and Willie and sit in at their regular meetings of the censorship staff: some-times by the night train, when I had time to take the ferry to Staten Island and back in the early morning before beginning work; sometimes by air, when I could look down on the French liner *Normandie* lying sadly on her side in the harbour. At the theatre in New York I saw a play in which C. Aubrey Smith was appearing; he was a brother-in-law of one of my most beloved New Court friends, Algy Wood, and I went round to have a drink with him in his dressing-room afterwards. The long string attaching me to NMR was tugged by Evelyn Baring, who came to Washington and brought me news of the firm; and by my chief, Bobbie Stopford, who flew home for a short visit and promised not only to convey my respectful greetings to Anthony, whom he knew, but also, with a kindly eye to my post-war prospects, to tell him what 'a grand job' I was doing.

The delicious spring came and went in a flash and the hot and humid summer enveloped us, a summer for which I had prepared myself by the purchase of Palm Beach suits and a broad-brimmed straw hat. I found plenty of exercise by playing tennis on the Ambassador's court, sometimes with H.E. himself, and swimming in his pool. June brought my thirty-fourth birth-day and a chocolate cake from the stenographers of the section. It also saw a polite mutiny which with equal politeness we had to quash: the same stenographers, Canadians to a girl, whose duties included that of making tea in the afternoon, sought to wean us from a habit which seemed to them crazy in that weather and to substitute iced Coca-Cola for which a convenient dispensing machine had been installed.

In August I had a seaside holiday at Bethany Beach on the coast of Delaware. In October, unhappily, Bill Wade was sum-moned back to London by the Treasury. The faithful Mary, who after several months' devoted service confessed to having a husband and a child, stayed on contentedly: she had become a confirmed Anglophile as a result, I hope, partly of working for two Englishmen but more perhaps of reports from her husband and other coloured American soldiers of their friendly reception by people in England.

The Washington episode and its aftermath in London, which together kept me away from New Court until January 1946, constituted an experience which was of intense interest to me for a number of reasons. It gave me valuable knowledge of the Whitehall machine and its methods; it taught me a great deal about the way the American governmental system worked; and it enabled me to meet, and in some cases to know well, men then in mid-career whose subsequent climb to top positions and appearance in the honours list I watched with pleasure. First and Second Secretaries rose to become knights and ambassadors, some to leave the service and adorn the boards of merchant banks and industrial companies or to direct universities and colleges. One such colleague went downhill: before I left Washington Donald Maclean arrived in the Chancery but although I frequently saw him around I had little official or social contact with him.

One man among the interesting figures who worked in the Embassy in those war-time years or who came for brief periods and were quickly gone stands out above all others as possessed of the most powerful and fascinating mind with which I have ever come into contact. A privilege and pleasure which I treasured beyond measure was to read the file of political telegrams which was circulated to those who I understand from the work of John Le Carré are known in some quarters as 'dips'. Although no doubt the file was edited by somebody before it reached my desk and 'top secret' papers were removed which it was neither necessary nor desirable for me to see, it still contained enough telegrams originating in, or addressed or repeated to, Washington, to give an absorbing glimpse of other corners of the diplomatic battle-field. I remember, for example, the wonderful series of long signals in which Sir Samuel Hoare told the Foreign Office, rather complacently I thought, of his talks with General Franco in Madrid. But the telegram I looked forward to and enjoyed most was the weekly political summary, often two or three foolscap pages in length, which kept H.M.G. informed of the trends of public and newspaper opinion in America and of political views and attitudes in Congress and other circles. This report seemed to me, and indeed was generally agreed, to be quite brilliantly done. The typed copies which I saw bore a string of initials indicating the men who had contributed to or amended or approved the telegrams; the 'H' which came first stood for the Ambassador and at the end, as the *fons et origo* 'IB' denoted the man primarily responsible for the drafting. His name was Isaiah Berlin.

These political summaries, which I admired as much for their stylistic elegance as for their illuminating content, were highly appreciated in Whitehall, not least by the Prime Minister himself, who prayed to be told the name of the author. Shortly afterwards, hearing that Mr I. Berlin had arrived in London on a visit, he caused him to be invited to lunch and it was not until they had been talking at cross purposes for several minutes that it was discovered that the guest was Irving and not Isaiah.

Sir Isaiah, as he very properly now is, was an Oxford don who had been working for the Ministry of Information in New York and came to Washington in 1942. Since he is unlikely now to have either the time or the inclination to read anything so light and trivial as this narrative I need not fear to embarrass him by recording the intellectual pleasure which I derived from his society. We frequently lunched together in the canteen and the memories I have of his scintillating conversation and massive erudition are among the most delightful that I retain of that memorable interlude. He told me later that for him, too, the years in Washington were some of the most agreeable of his life, but no doubt the reason is very different.

Chapter 12 Sees and Jays

By the summer of 1944 we were all beginning to anticipate the end of the war and to wonder how long it would be before we were released to find new seats to sit in or return to old ones that were being kept warm for us. Bobbie Stopford, considering that his section could run well enough without him and that we might as well in future report direct to Noel Hall, the Minister in charge, had gone home to become Deputy Director of Civil Affairs at the War Office. The President of a big American lumber company whom I had met while on holiday in Vermont and visited in New York threw out strong hints that there would be a job for me in his organization if I wanted it. Instigated and accompanied by Willie Hill-Wood, a partner in J. P. Morgan & Co. gave me lunch at the Bankers Club in Wall Street, told me that one of their biggest customers, an engineering company, was planning to open an office in London after the war and asked if I would like to be considered for the post of its London representative. There was talk of the conditions under which temporary 'dips', if they so desired and were considered suitable, could become permanently established. But for me the call of New Court was irresistible. My modest ambition was to be head of the Dividend Office, a position for which I had been trained, which I felt I could hold down satisfactorily and for which I was the only candidate in sight.

However, another eighteen months were to pass before NMR

and I were reunited. In the meantime the authorities had agreed that as soon as a seat in a plane could be found for me I could fly home for two or three weeks for talks in the Ministry in which I had spent only five days three years ago. The booking came through simultaneously with the appearance in the American papers of terrifying stories from London about robot bombers or pilotless planes. It would have required more courage to cancel my passage than to go as planned and in July, concealing my nervousness as best I could, I departed from Baltimore by clipper. The comfortable and roomy flying-boat lumbered up to Botwood in Newfoundland, which was wearing its smiling summer face, and then across to Foynes in southern Eire, whence a small blacked-out plane took us to Hendon. Late in the evening I arrived in the accustomed inky darkness at the Connaught Hotel to spend much of the night under the bed listening to the alarming rumble of the V.1's and the even more alarming silence when their engines cut out.

At the other side of Berkeley Square, in M.E.W., they had already got used to this new horror and with a calmness which I could not emulate scarcely looked up from their desks when the contemptuously named 'doodle-bugs' were heard. I was ashamed of the relief I felt when I left to spend a week in the rural tranquillity of Market Drayton, where my mother lived, and of the still greater relief when I got safely away on my return flight. We came down at Baltimore in the stifling heat of an August afternoon. Alan Watt, a friend from the Australian Legation, was at the seaplane base to meet Sir Howard Florey of penicillin fame and saved me a sticky train journey by giving me a lift in his car to Washington.

Now the sands were running out quickly. Three months after my return a signal arrived from the Foreign Office inviting me to wind up the affairs I was handling in Washington and fly back to London with all convenient speed to take up a completely new and different job in the Control Office for Germany and Austria. I was to become a principal attaché to the Economic Advisory Branch of the Foreign Office and to work on post-war economic planning for Austria. This was a country of which I knew little or nothing; I ransacked the Embassy library for books on the subject which I tried hurriedly to study while I was packing and tidying up and while the Travel Section were trying to squeeze me into an aeroplane. In December, after a few hours at Gander in Labrador, one of the most desolate and in mid-winter iciest spots on earth, a little party of us took off in a converted Liberator clutching flying suits and oxygen masks in case, as I was told happened not infrequently, the heating or the pressurization broke down. In fact we were warm and reasonably comfortable, and although we were packed in so tightly that the flying-boat seemed as spacious as a Pullman train in comparison, we crossed the Atlantic in little more than half the time. Another interlude was over.

In London I found myself back in Berkeley Square; not in Berkeley Square House, where the rump of M.E.W. was being wound up, but in Lansdowne House, a block of luxury flats on the south side. There I entered into occupation not just of an office, which had been the living-room of a flat, but also of the bare bones of a kitchenette and a small bathroom. There I rejoined Bill Ritchie who had preceded me into an adjoining suite and was now an Assistant Secretary, this step ahead of me having been necessitated, as he was careful to explain lest I should feel jealous, by the circumstance of his opposite number among the rank-conscious Russians being a major-general. I met our small but select and highly skilled staff of executive officers, clerks and typists. Above all I was introduced to the remarkable man in charge who directed operations where he did not actually carry them out himself. The first thing he told me was that I was not going to work on Austria, after all, but on Germany.

This ball-of-fire, now well known in the City as Sir Mark Turner, a managing director of Kleinwort Benson Ltd, the merchant bankers, and chairman or director of a number of great public companies, had arisen from a comparatively lowly position in M.E.W. to be the king-pin of post-war economic planning for Germany and Austria. Tall and thin like me, he had unlike me a seemingly inexhaustible fund of nervous energy and a financial brain of astonishing range and penetration. His charm of manner made him an agreeable boss to work for, although he was also a somewhat frustrating one by reason of his habit of doing most of the work himself and delegating no more of it than he was obliged to. In my case this was probably just as well: although the experience I had gained with NMR and in Washington was certainly useful and although I also brought to the job what I fancied was a certain ability as a draftsman, these hardly compensated for a lack of basic economic training. However, it was gratifying to find that there was some reluctance to release me when the war was over and Sir Alexander Cadogan, then Permanent Under-Secretary of State for Foreign Affairs, himself signed a 'dear Tony' letter to his old friend Anthony de Rothschild urging him to allow me to remain in the service for a while. Anthony agreed that my return to New Court should be postponed until 1 January 1946. This, I was both glad and sorry to note, considerably disappointed Brooks, who, Bev wrote, was 'crying out' for me.

The intervening months, full of interest, long hours of work, committee meetings and occasional panics caused by the dreaded pink 'PQ' flags denoting Parliamentary questions passed quickly. Our band provided the headquarters staff, and Mark the chairman, of a body called the Economic and Industrial Planning Staff, generally referred to by the acronym 'EIPS' which was pronounced to rhyme with 'swipes'. We did not remain very long in Lansdowne House and when we moved to Norfolk House, St James's Square, I permitted myself to signalize our change of address by the following lines which were composed one afternoon after lunch in the smoking-room of the Travellers' Club:

> We are going up in the temporal world,
> We can say without fear of rebuke,
> For Lansdowne was only a marquess
> But Norfolk a gartered duke:

And our spiritual progress also
Shows us pure and free from taint,
For Berkeley was only a bishop
But James a blessed saint.

The New Court to which I went back in January 1946 after
an effective absence of more than six years was outwardly the
same New Court that I had left in September 1939. It stood,
only slightly battered, in the midst of acres of devastation and
we who returned were only too thankfully aware that if the
building had not been still there our jobs might not have been
there either. That we were welcomed back, however, was due
not only to the fact that New Court had providentially escaped
a direct hit, from which no devoted guards could have pre-
served it, but to the fortitude of two men in particular, Anthony
de Rothschild and Hugh Davies.

The strain which the sole surviving partner must have been
under while he guided the firm through its most difficult years
can easily be imagined and the effect of it on his health became
all too clear in the ensuing years. It would not be surprising to
learn that he was sometimes tempted to give up; whether or not
he ever was is known only to his family and perhaps also to
others who then or later were in the inmost councils. What is
certain is that he would not have been able to carry on as he did
and to hand over a thriving and expanding business to his successors if Hugh Davies had not been at his side to share the
burden and support and sustain him. The many new men who
have now found rewarding and absorbing careers with a firm
which has not just recaptured its old glory but has risen to new
heights of fame owe more than they realize to a man they never
knew, a man but for whose courage and endurance none of this
might have happened.

Before the war I had known Hugh as Steph's right hand, who
sat with us in the Old Room through many of our protracted
tussles or who sometimes just dropped in to take two puffs at a
du Maurier before extinguishing it in Sir William Goode's
silver ashtray. He was a man in whom human kindness

over-flowed; no matter what one's personal problem was he was never too busy to spend time discussing and solving it. After the war we became much closer. He found me a flat in the same block as his own and we used to travel to and from the office together whenever possible, a practice which I like to think was due as much to mutual affection as to the incipient illness which made him reluctant to brave the tube alone.

But the breakdown of his health was still in the unforeseen future when we came together again after the war, with Hugh and Michael Bucks running the office as General Manager and Assistant General Manager and Harry Brooks and me as No. 1 and No. 2 in the D.O. In 1947 we floated public issues for Town Tailors Ltd of Leeds and for Cussons. Hugh took me with him on a visit to the Cussons factory in Salford, where we lunched with Alexander Cussons, their founder, and his sons and watched grandmothers who had joined as young girls working in a fog of talcum powder with no other effect on them than to give them the most beautiful complexions.

No more delightful a companion than Hugh on an expedition of this sort could be imagined. He taught me a great deal and his conversation was always leavened with dry humour. It was about this time that NMR put a considerable amount of money into the development of a process for the manufacture of a chipboard bonded with resin, called 'plimber'. When Shamah, its inventor, was describing one day the completely automatic plant which he had designed to make it, in which one had only to press a button here for this and another there for that, Hugh said: 'Well, I hope there's a button B somewhere which NMR can press.'

His wit was often of a paronomastic kind and when Bev came up from Tring during the war, as he frequently did for a couple of days to see his barber and his chiropodist, Hugh greeted him with: 'Ah, Bev—hair today and corns tomorrow?' I also heard with pleasure that he was not too hard pressed in those strenuous days to display some cunning for his own benefit. Anthony, ever public-spirited, had instructed the butler that cod should be the staple diet in his dining-room and as a consequence, to Hugh's disgust, that uninteresting fish also regularly appeared on the managers' table. Hugh succeeded in changing this regimen by persuading Anthony that an even greater public spirit would be shown if turbot or Dover sole were eaten by everyone who could afford it, leaving the available supplies of cod for those who could not.

That iron man, Harry Brooks, as hale and eupeptic as ever, who had been calling for me insistently and was flatteringly glad to have me back at his side, was another who had been carrying on resolutely through anxious times and whose strong support had never failed in spite of the personal tragedy which the war had inflicted on him. Almost single-handed he had been responsible for the reorganization on a permanent basis of the entire Brazilian long-term sterling debt, the management of which I inherited. I was back in time to help him with a similar operation for Chile into which we were soon plunged; happily plunged, so far as I was concerned, for this was the kind of work, detailed and technical, for which I had been trained and which I felt thoroughly understood. A small mission came over from Chile to negotiate the settlement with us: the two principals, of whom we saw most, were Solminihac, an expert from the Chilean National Debt Office, and his leader Vergara, a high civil servant who later became Minister of Finance and never failed when he was in London to invite me to the Chilean Embassy and remember with an affectionate hug the months we had spent toiling amicably together. I was back in an old familiar world as we sat round the table, with Hilary Scott as our legal adviser, drafting and revising contracts and offers to bondholders and the consequential forms and press announcements.

In 1948, near the date of my fortieth birthday, I was given a 'per procuration' signature. At the end of 1949 Brooks retired and went with his wife on a visit to Chile at the invitation of the Chilean Government. On 1 January 1950 I became Head of the D.O., which was still the largest division in New Court, and entered the surtax bracket.

Anthony de Rothschild continued to rule benignly over all. He was still only sixty in 1947 and there was no outward sign of the toll which his brother's death and the years of strain and anxiety had taken of his health. He did not suffer fools much more gladly than before; there were still occasional painful flashes of the old impatience and his sense of humour, though more strongly in evidence, was still unpredictable. When my old friend Hawes was sent on a mission to Tangier I remarked that this was rather like sending Miss Coles, one of the senior secretaries, to Newcastle. The apophthegm pleased me, was well received throughout New Court and is still remembered; but when it was repeated to Anthony it fell, I was told, remarkably flat. However, there is no doubt that the years had mellowed him to an extent which I should not have thought possible. To me he was an almost totally different man. I ran into him in Berkeley Square while I was working there and mourned with him the loss of his beautiful house in Hill Street near by, which had been destroyed by bombing; he was cheerful and optimistic, interested to hear what I was doing and how soon I expected to get back to New Court. And after my return he would ring me on the house telephone instead of imperiously pressing the bell which summoned me to his presence and pull my leg and laugh. He called upon me for help with *The Times* crossword puzzle on days when he had been unable to finish it in the train. When I told him that Sir Roger Stevens, now Vice-Chancellor of Leeds University but then an Assistant Under-Secretary of State at the Foreign Office, had telephoned me to ask if I could go back for a few months to help with the drafting of the satellite peace treaties he said coldly: 'Well, obviously you can't, can you?' But his eyes were smiling.

He began to invite me from time to time to concern myself with him in all sorts of matters, both official and unofficial, that were not strictly within my province. The most notable example of this occurred when, following the first visit to New Court of Premier Joseph Smallwood of Newfoundland, he asked me to be present at the subsequent talks which led to the formation of the British Newfoundland Corporation. So far as this involved the staff it was really the baby of my old friend and contemporary Peter Hobbs, who had become the firm's Investment

Manager. But Anthony, already foreseeing, as only a few others did, the gigantic oak that would grow from this small acorn, realized that its cultivation would require more work than could be performed by one man. The story of the birth and early years of this great enterprise, which is also an example of Anthony's far-sightedness and of the romantic adventurousness which can exist in the staid and conservative bosoms of modern merchant bankers, has been told elsewhere. It is only necessary to say that Brinco thenceforward dominated my life to such an extent that I had eventually to be detached almost completely from the D.O. to devote myself to it, a preoccupation which did not cease when I became Secretary of the bank. It took me to Canada a dozen times in the space of a few years and remains not only by far the biggest but also the most interesting and exciting affair that I was ever engaged in on NMR's behalf.

At lunch one New Year's Day during the period of struggle and disappointment and refusal to be daunted we were all asked to give our 'nap' selection, in any field we liked, for the coming year. I plumped for Brinco, which showed more confidence than prescience, for I was ante-dating success by several years. 'It may be your "nap",' Peter said instantly, 'but it keeps me awake.'

The hard work and frequent anxieties which were my lot at this time were immeasurably sweetened by the warmer personal relationship that I began to establish with Anthony. Nobody who had not experienced life at New Court in the old days and worked on the hither side of the great gulf that separated the partners from even the most senior members of their staff, a gulf of which vestiges still exist although numerous bridges have been thrown across it, could have appreciated how great and refreshing was the change. What we were witnessing was a part of the New Court revolution.

The last time I saw Anthony was a few months before his death in February 1961, several years after a stroke had removed him from New Court and put an end to all his activities. It was customary for two cricket matches to take place each summer, one at Exbury in May when the rhododendrons were at their best and the other later in the year at

Anthony's country home, Ascott House, at Wing, near Leighton Buzzard, when a team from New Court played the local eleven and the staff were invited down to watch the game, take lunch in the pavilion and look at the garden. In 1926 I myself was a member of the New Court side at Ascott, the only occasion since leaving school on which I have attempted to play cricket except with a soft ball on the sand of the sea-shore; one catch held and a score of nought not out did not seem to justify me in putting my name down again. But I enjoyed the gardens, the wild woodlands and the lush profusion of rhododendrons and azaleas at Exbury as much as the quite different formal parterres and smooth lawns at Ascott, from which one looked across the unspoiled green valley to Mentmore. As I walked round on that warm Sunday afternoon I was thinking, naturally enough, of Anthony, and suddenly there he was, fifty yards away, sitting in his wheelchair and attended by a nurse. I had the impression that a second before he had told her to stop.

The brim of his hat was turned down and the lower part of his face was swathed in a woollen scarf. Between them his eyes seemed to be peering at me with something of the old keenness. I did not know if he recognized me or was well enough to talk to me or would have wanted to do so. It was a strange and regrettable thing that throughout his illness we at New Court who held him in such affection had found the greatest difficulty in getting news of him. I knew that one or two men, closer to him than I, had been to see him and that there had even been times when they were allowed to show him official papers and discuss business with him. But no bulletins were issued: although such a proceeding might have been rejected as treating him too much like a member of the Royal Family or a distinguished statesman it was apparently not realized that the concern felt for him in our small world was no different from that of the people at large for a national leader.

I hesitated uncertainly, stopped and turned sadly away.

Although that was the last time I saw him, I prefer to remember him as he was on a joyous occasion before he was stricken.

In February 1955 his daughter Renée was married to Peter Robeson at the church of All Saints, Wing. A few of us were invited to the wedding and to the reception afterwards at Ascott House. As he moved smiling among his guests, temporarily forgetting his responsibilities and not yet threatened by the creeping shadow of his coming illness, the picture he presented was one of positive joviality. I shall remember it always as a true picture, too; its only flaw was that it was not painted in fast colours.

The twenty years following the end of the war were for NMR the years of revolution. The changes did not begin in 1945 nor did they end in 1965; the process which began almost imperceptibly is still continuing. But between those dates the really epochal breaks with the past took place: the death of Anthony de Rothschild, the admission as partners of men who were not members of or even related to the Rothschild family, and the demolition of the old New Court and its replacement by an entirely new building.

The new partners were drawn from the ranks of New Court itself as well as from outside; in the latter case the radical departure from tradition looked and sounded rather better in a Spanish-language newspaper's reference to *una persona enteramente de fuera* than in Joseph Wechsberg's *ein absoluter Outsider*.

Less obviously newsworthy but not to be ignored were other changes which NMR underwent in common with other merchant banks. The number of bodies increased rapidly and significantly in the post-war years. It was no longer practicable for new entrants to be conducted round the office and introduced to everybody. Increasingly one saw faces about to which one could not put a name, a normal experience in any big organization but strange to the older generation at New Court, who used to know all their colleagues and most of them very well.

As a natural result of the big rise in numbers there was also an increase in the number of managers who were required or entitled to lunch on the premises. Hugh Davies had long been complaining that the noise level in the dining-room was approaching that in the parrot-house at the Zoo owing to the number of women who ate there at the same time as he did, although at a separate table. Eventually the din reached such a pitch that he could no longer hear himself or his neighbours speak and the entertainment of guests became virtually impossible. He rebelled and annexed the housekeeper's room as a dining-room for himself and the seven or eight senior managers. In that apartment, which was also in the basement and had no windows, we at least found peace and quiet, if not surroundings of noticeably greater elegance. After I moved into Chetwynd House, as recorded later, I was allowed to commission Austen Hall, the architect of that building, to beautify the room for us. It was a difficult assignment but he carried it out so successfully that our dining-room acquired the name of the 'Velvet Room', while the old one thereafter became known as the 'Cottage Tea-room' in spite of the absence of the chintz and fake Jacobean furniture which the appellation suggested.

The proportion of females to males increased; women were employed more and more, not only as secretaries and typists and manipulators of coupons but also in clerical and minor executive, if not yet in managerial, posts. Business expanded in traditional fields and into new ones, branches were opened at home and subsidiaries or affiliates established abroad. The use of machines of various kinds increased. Advertising was resorted to more frequently and more imaginatively. The firm's name appeared often enough in prospectuses and announcements to bondholders, it used to be thought, for little more to be necessary than an occasional bald statement of our name and address in special supplements issued by the more dignified dailies or in favoured weeklies such as the *Jewish Chronicle* and *The Economist*. After the war the practice grew of designing advertisements specifically to attract new clients for the various services which we offered and of publishing them in a wider selection of journals. The method of recruiting staff changed. In the past, young men were usually, although not invariably, engaged direct from school, either as the result of personal introductions or because they were the sons or nephews of existing employees, and were given a general training before settling down more or less permanently to the kind of work for which they seemed best fitted. Latterly it was found necessary to supplement this system by taking on older men with university degrees or qualifications in, for example, law or accountancy to fill particular vacancies.

It will not be supposed that all these changes were welcomed by all those who lived through them. Feelings about them ranged from universal pleasure at the decision to open the partnership to members of the staff to universal grief at the death of Anthony, which was of course different in kind from all the others. I must not exaggerate the extent to which I was in his confidence during his last years at New Court and it would be quite wrong to suggest that we ever became close friends or approached anything resembling intimacy. Nevertheless I did get to know him well enough to venture the opinion that if he had not died when he did the fundamental changes at New Court which I have mentioned would not have taken place, or not at the same time or in the same way. He would not, I feel sure, have taken kindly to the much more competitive world in which merchant bankers can no longer sit and wait for business to be brought to them but must actively seek it by advertising, which he thought vulgar, or by dashing constantly about in aeroplanes. He scorned to cultivate men whom he did not particularly like for the sake of possibly valuable contacts. He did not travel himself and he did not sit on the boards of the numerous public companies which would have been delighted to have him. 'They know where we live,' he would say of potential clients; 'if they want to do business with us let them come and talk to us.' And when they did come, if he did not like their faces or their manners he showed them the door without hesitation, no matter how profitable the proposed transaction might be.

Nor would he have had much patience with young men who were not content to start at the bottom and work their way up but wanted the posts and salaries of executives from the word go and, moreover, the assurance that the highest positions in the firm were open to them. He was too intellectually honest to have been found defending the hereditary system in the abstract, although he himself was a beneficiary of it and was in some respects, like other members of the family, the prisoner of his own upbringing. Hereditary titles are a slightly comic irrelevance, like costermongers' pearlies; hereditary money and property are comforts which we should all like to receive and pass on and are in moderation harmless: but the inheritance without other qualifications of power over people's lives is no longer tolerable or defensible. All this Anthony must have known and, as we have seen, he himself was far from incapable of adapting himself to new ideas and new conditions. Nevertheless I cannot help feeling that the pace at least, if not the actual steps, of the changes at New Court would have been different if he had lived.

About the third major change, the rebuilding of the office, which certainly marked the end of an era in a concrete and unmistakable way, feelings were mixed and opinions divided. Not that anyone doubted the necessity of doing something radical: the old building presented a physical bar to expansion less easy to surmount than the moral obstacle of inelastic minds. The pressure inside was mounting to such an extent that the fanciful could almost see the fortress walls beginning to bulge and crack like those of a boiler with the safety valve screwed down. Tinkering could go no further. Already a new storey had been built over the Dividend Office, rooms with high ceilings had been divided horizontally and individual *lebensraum* pared to the limit. In 1956 we overflowed across St Swithin's Lane and most of the D.O., myself included, was moved to Chetwynd House, a new building which had arisen opposite New Court where formerly the City Carlton Club and a row of shops had faced us. Gone was the City Carlton, which I passed twice a day but never in my life entered, a club which would have been so handy for New Court clubmen if they had not found all the amenities they wanted on their own side of the lane; gone were the ABC where some of us drank tea for a change in the afternoon, Mrs Butchart's flower shop which supplied wreaths for funerals and roses for girl-friends or neglected wives, and Prestat's where we bought truffles for secretaries' birthdays.

For the D.O. the move was only the first of a series of upheavals to which it was subjected during the years that followed. We were consoled by the fact that the move was one of only a few yards, leaving us still well in sight of home; I myself was mollified by being comfortably installed in a new room not a whit smaller or less handsome than the Old Room which I had left. My windows were right on the street instead of overlooking the quiet courtyard, but fortunately the traffic was light. Wheeled traffic, that is; pedestrian traffic was quite another matter. During the morning and evening rush-hours thousands of City workers tramped along St Swithin's Lane on their way from or to the stations in Cannon Street; at these times persons wishing to cross from Chetwynd House to New Court or vice versa had to plunge into the striding throng as into a fast-running stream and were lucky if they were not carried a long way down before they could get over and jostle their way back against the current on the other side.

But all these measures proved to be merely palliatives. The question became not whether to rebuild but where. Was the old address at which NMR had been doing business for more than 150 years and which was familiar to banking circles throughout the world so valuable that we must rebuild on the same site despite the limitations imposed by its restricted area and by the City planning authorities? So said those swayed by the powerful imponderables of sentiment, tradition and a sense of historical continuity. No, said others; that was not sentiment but sentimentalism. What mattered was not where you lived but the efficiency of the service you could give your clients. If accommodation could be found elsewhere in the City spacious enough not only for immediate needs but for those of the foreseeable future, and if it was clear that thereby efficient operation would be promoted and expansion facilitated, good-bye should be said to New Court, St Swithin's Lane, without a pang.

As the whole world now knows, or at any rate that section of it which is interested in such matters, the proponents of the former view prevailed. No doubt it was a difficult decision to make and more complex considerations were involved than those I have adumbrated. In 1962 the demolition gangs began work. From the day when the first sledge-hammers swung in the hands of the wreckers to that on which the heavy glass doors swung to admit the public, wide-eyed and wondering, to the new New Court, a period of two years and nine months elapsed. To the simple-minded the interval and our displacement during it were no more than the corollary of the decision to pull down the old building and erect another in its place. For others they had a numinous significance. Souls departing this life in a state of grace nevertheless required to be purged from venial sins in a place of temporary suffering and expiation. The name of the particular purgatory to which we were consigned pending heaven was City Gate House.

This unbeautiful pile stood on the south side of Finsbury Square in surroundings which, although only a mile separated them from St Swithin's Lane, were all too clearly beyond the pale of the City. They seemed as different from our accustomed haunts as the vulgar sweat and litter of Les Halles from the ordered dignity of the Place Vendôme. The offices and shops looked for the most part smaller and shabbier, the people less well-dressed, the struggle to make a living more nakedly evident. It was a place of commerce and industry rather than of banking and insurance and similar genteel pursuits, of pullovers and shirt-sleeves rather than of white collars and black hats. In our sheltered life to the south we had been unused to the din and fumes of buses and lorries passing rudely before our windows or to buying our tobacco at shops which also sold candy, ice-cream and newspapers. However, Finsbury Square itself, it must be admitted, did have a sort of blowzy charm: its bowling-green and beds of lavender compensated a little for the café and the petrol pumps and particularly in summer, when girls in gay dresses sat in deck-chairs or lay on the grass, sunning themselves and listening to the brass band which sometimes played in the lunch-hour, it presented a colourful and lively spectacle to the eye of the exile.

At last, in July 1965, our dream of dwelling in marble halls came true. We girded up our loins, endured again, this time with hope and gladness, the dusty and wearying horrors of packing and unpacking, and began the process of settling into our new home. It was the dawn of a new era.

My story now is ended. I have tried to draw an impressionistic picture of an office and the way life was lived in it because they have both now vanished for ever, because they were unique and because I look back on them with nostalgic affection. I have tried to describe the transformation of a great nineteenth-century firm into a great modern one, not as a piece of economic history but from the point of view of one who lived through it. I have not written about the present New Court because it is there for all who are interested to see, or about the business as it is conducted today because in that respect NMR no longer differs fundamentally from its major competitors. If I have dwelt too lovingly on the past it is not because the fascination it has for me blinds me to the shortcomings and imperfections which made changes not so much desirable as essential for survival. As I trod the carpeted corridors of the new edifice I may have been heard softly wailing 'Ichabod, Ichabod', but even in our old home I was now and then constrained to recite fervently the fourth verse of the 123rd Psalm. It is possible to argue about the details of the changes but not that changes were necessary. New Court could not have stood still.

The conscientious attempt to keep my private life out of the story, and to relate only such of my own doings as were connected, even if indirectly, with New Court has not been wholly successful. In any case the last scene must be of myself as Secretary of the firm, when the fortieth anniversary of my induction has come and gone and the years have begun to succeed one another with bewildering rapidity. A mind into which thoughts of *otium cum dignitate* have begun to creep is gratified to find itself not wholly drained of creative energy and with enough elasticity to turn to matters wholly different in kind from any that have come its way officially before.

The post of Secretary of NMR conjured up in the minds of

outsiders a picture of a Hankey, a Bridges or a Normanbrook performing for the partners in conference assembled the services which those eminent but self-effacing civil servants rendered to the Cabinet. I was referred to, again by an outsider, as New Court's *éminence grise*. But in fact only the epithet was accurate and the picture quite false. The Secretary, as the job had developed since its creation by Anthony in the thirties for the specific purpose of the firm's charitable activities, was concerned with everything except banking. He certainly continued to deal with charitable appeals, which he both received and issued; but in addition he drafted speeches and articles, answered general inquiries of every imaginable kind, entertained visiting firemen, lectured occasionally, represented the firm on committees and at meetings and functions, sat through interminable dinners and was rewarded from time to time with an expensive seat at a Royal *première*. The firm was continually involved in a wide variety of affairs that had no, or only a remote, connection with banking; when anything turned up that did not fit into any other department it landed on the Secretary's plate. His work, at any rate during my term of office, was political, diplomatic, literary, artistic, even philosophical—anything but financial. Above all he was concerned with Jewish affairs. It was an almost everyday occurrence for me to find myself the only Christian—indeed the only non-Jew—in an otherwise completely homogeneous gathering, and furthermore to be welcomed in a manner that I never felt was wholly due to the fact that I was there as the representative of leaders of the Anglo-Jewish community.

There was another reason for my happiness in this new world. My translation to it coincided with my perhaps belated recognition that I did not possess the kind of financial brain that merchant banking in the modern age demanded. The day of the professional had arrived and I was, after all, an amateur. It was no longer possible for intricate financial operations to be negotiated and planned by the general managers of the office and the managers of the D.O. while their regular work was set temporarily aside or in nocturnal sessions. They came along now so thick and fast and were so complex and protracted that it had been necessary to set up a new Finance Department to deal with them and to staff it with professional experts in law and accountancy and allied skills. I said good-bye with some regret to the fiscal agencies, particularly that of the Royal Dutch Petroleum Company, which I had nursed with assiduous devotion; with relief to the take-over battles which I neither liked nor fully understood. Of all the concerns of my previous existence only Brinco remained, a lusty young giant now but not too big or too proud to call from time to time for the advice of the assistant midwife who helped to bring him into the world.

The internal telephone rings on my desk. It is HMV. The senior partner and senior Rothschild has, as usual, a number of irons in the fire which I help him to keep hot. It may be desalination and nuclear reactors or the affairs of Israel, which I have visited with him several times; perhaps he has to deliver a major speech or is wondering how to raise more money for the Central British Fund or the Council of Christians and Jews; or maybe another chapter in the Brinco saga is about to be written. Whatever it is, he likes to try out his ideas on me and dictate in my presence rough and rapid drafts which I can afterwards turn into what he is pleased to call 'Palinese'. Now I am invited to 'pop up' to his room and bring my secretary with me. 'Dearly beloved Joanna, I pray and beseech you to accompany me with a pure heart and humble voice. . . .'